UNDERSTANDING THE IMMIGRATION BAN, INDIVIDUAL'S REACTIONS *AND* LEGAL BATTLE

Edited by
Gerald N Okonkwo

Copyrighted Material

Copyright ©2017 by G.N Okonkwo
ISBN- 13: 978-1544633978

All rights reversed.

No part of this publication maybe reproduced, stored in retrieval system, or transmitted in any form or by any means, electronic, mechanical, photocopying, recording or otherwise without the prior written permission of the editor or publisher (Createspace publishing resources).

Contact:
Website: www.createspace.com

Contents

Introduction   5

Sections

1. **The Executive Order**   7
    Brief History and examples of Executive order
    Executive orders are controversial
    Congressional Recourse
    Difference between an Executive order and an Executive Action
    Presidential Proclamation
    Presidential Memorandum
    Presidential Directives
    Executive Order No 13769 Protecting The Nation From Foreign Terrorist Entering into The United State. (Full text of Immigration Travel Ban)

    Constitutional Backing
    Where The Idea Came From
    What the Immigrants need to know about Trump's order
    Legal Battle Begin
    Legality Questioned
    US Court Refuses to Reinstate Trump's Immigration Ban

2. People's Reactions
    Trump Travel Ban is Anti-Muslim Fear Mongering new Law suit says

    Precedent to This Ban
    Others Dispute Trump's Contention that this Order is Similar To Obama's Order

    The Ban's Christian Focus
    White House Chief of Staff Reince Priebus's Opinion
    Mark Zuckerberg responds on trump travel ban
    Malala Yousafzai responds on trump travel ban
    U.S Senator John McCain says President Trump's travel ban will "Give ISIS some more propaganda"

    Grand old Party (GOP) Criticism
    What some of Catholic leaders said about Trump's travel Ban
    What World leaders have to say on Donald Trump's 'Travel Ban'
    UN Experts Say Trump Travel Ban Illegal Endanger Refugees
    Professional NASCAR racer Dale Earnhardt Jr. Publicly Denounced President Trump's Muslim ban

    The LAPD Police Chief Openly Rebelled against Trump's Immigration Orders

    Dan Rather Went Viral Responding to Trump's Refugee Ban

The ACLU Sued Trump
Angelina Jolie Just Responded To Trump's Travel Ban
Mark Cuban Blasted Trump's "Half-Baked" Muslim Ban
Federal Courts Give Conflicting Directions on Travel Ban

Introduction

With just a few quick strokes of the pen, President Donald Trump on Friday 27th January 2017 banned -- temporarily, for now -- roughly 218 million people from entering the United States.

Trump barred citizens of seven Muslim-majority countries from entering the US for at least the next 90 days by executive order, which a senior White House official said later Friday is likely just a first step toward establishing a broader ban.
Its unclear how many more countries will be added to the list, but the official said the administration will be "very aggressive" as it weighs how many more countries to add to the list.
Asked what criteria the administration will consider as it looks to expand the ban beyond the initial seven countries, the official said simply the "mandate is to keep America safe."
"Not going to take any risks," the official added.
That's just one part of the controversial executive order Trump signed Friday dubbed: "Protecting the nation from foreign terrorist entry into the United States." Many of the provisions in the order are consistent with Trump's campaign pledges.
Here's a breakdown of what the executive order does.
Trump banned citizens of seven Muslim-majority countries from entering the US for at least the next 90 days.
The executive order bars all people hailing from Iraq, Syria, Iran, Libya, Somalia, Sudan and Yemen -- or at least 218 million people, based on 2015 data published by the World Bank -- from entering the United States. Those countries were named in a 2016 law concerning immigration visas as "countries of concern."
But the executive order also makes clear those seven countries are just a starting point for a likely broader ban.
The order exempts diplomats and members of international organizations from the ban.
The order also directs the secretary of Homeland Security to conduct a 30-day review to determine which countries do not provide "adequate information" for its citizens to be issued visas to enter the US.
During the campaign, Trump talked about these countries as "terror-prone" countries. During the GOP primary campaign, he called for banning all Muslims from the US -- a statement he never retracted -- before shifting toward calling for banning individuals from countries with terrorist links, though he never specified the countries.
Trump also stopped the admission of all refugees to the United States for four months.

During that time, Trump's secretary of state will review the application and screening process for refugees to be admitted to the US. The process is already highly rigorous and often takes successful refugee applicants at least two years to be admitted into the United States, but Trump has argued the program could still be exploited by terrorists.

Trump also more than halved the number of refugees who could eventually be admitted in 2017 to 50,000 from the 110,000 cap established under former President Barack Obama.

Trump also states in the order that refugees should be prioritized for entry on the basis of religious persecution, "provided that the religion of the individual is a minority religion." That would open the door for Christian refugees from Muslim-majority countries to be accepted in the US while Muslims fleeing those countries would be excluded.

"I hereby proclaim that the entry of nationals of Syria as refugees is detrimental to the interests of the United States and thus suspend any such entry," Trump declared in Friday's executive order.

While Trump during his campaign called for banning Syrian refugees from the US -- decrying their entry as a potential "Trojan horse" -- he also called for establishing a safe zone in Syria where Syrians fleeing the war-ravaged country could live peacefully. Trump made no mention of that plan in Friday's executive order, even though a draft of the executive order circulating in recent days called for beginning to plan for creating such zones.

The executive order also calls for the secretaries of state and homeland security, the director of national intelligence and the FBI director to develop and implement new immigration screening procedures.

The ban and its impact

Trump during his campaign called for developing new "extreme vetting" screening procedures that would weed out potential terrorists from visa applicants by asking questions about their views on the US and ensuring that individuals support the US's pluralistic values.

"In order to protect Americans, the United States must ensure that those admitted to this country do not bear hostile attitudes toward it and its founding principles," Trump states in the opening section of the executive order.

"The United States cannot, and should not, admit those who do not support the Constitution, or those who would place violent ideologies over American law. In addition, the United States should not admit those who engage in acts of bigotry or hatred...or those who would oppress Americans of any race, gender, or sexual orientation."

Gerald N Okonkwo

Executive orders:

FROM TIME TO TIME I HEAR THAT PRESIDENT BUSH HAS ISSUED AN EXECUTIVE ORDER ESTABLISHING THIS POLICY OR THAT. WHAT IS AN EXECUTIVE ORDER? WHERE DOES THE PRESIDENT GET THE AUTHORITY TO ISSUE THEM? IS THERE ANY WAY TO REVERSE AN EXECUTIVE ORDER?

Executive Orders (EOs) are legally binding orders given by the President, acting as the head of the Executive Branch, to Federal Administrative Agencies. Executive Orders are generally used to direct federal agencies and officials in their execution of congressionally established laws or policies. However, in many instances they have been used to guide agencies in directions contrary to congressional intent.

Not all EOs are created equal. Proclamations, for example, are a special type of Executive Order that are generally ceremonial or symbolic, such as when the President declares National Take Your Child To Work Day. Another subset of Executive Orders are those concerned with national security or defense issues. These have generally been known as National Security Directives. Under the Clinton Administration, they have been termed "Presidential Decision Directives."

Executive Orders do not require Congressional approval to take effect but they have the same legal weight as laws passed by Congress. The President's source of authority to issue Executive Orders can be found in the Article II, section 1 of the Constitution which grants to the President the "executive Power." Section 3 of Article II further directs the President to "take Care that the Laws be faithfully executed." To implement or execute the laws of the land, Presidents give direction and guidance to Executive Branch agencies and departments, often in the form of Executive Orders.

A Brief History and Examples

Executive Orders have been used by every chief executive since the time of George Washington. Most of these directives were unpublished and were only seen by the agencies involved. In the early 1900s, the State Department began numbering them; there are now over 13,000 numbered orders. Orders were retroactively numbered going back to 1862 when President Lincoln suspended the writ of habeas corpus and issued the Emancipation Proclamation by Executive Order. There are also many other Executive Orders that have not been numbered because they have been lost due to bad record-keeping. Such is not the problem today. All new Executive Orders are easily accessible.

Many important policy changes have occurred through Executive Orders. Harry Truman integrated the armed forces under Executive Order. President Eisenhower used an EO to desegregate schools. Presidents Kennedy and Johnson used them to bar racial discrimination in federal housing, hiring, and contracting. President Reagan used an EO to bar the use of federal funds for advocating abortion. President Clinton reversed this order when he came into office.

President Clinton has come under fire for using the EO as a way to make policy without consulting the Republican Congress (see the quotes at the beginning of this article). Clinton has signed over 300 EOs since 1992. In one case, he designated 1.7 million acres of Southern Utah as the Grant Staircase - Escalante National Monument. He also designated a system of American Heritage Rivers and even fought a war with Yugoslavia under Executive Order.

Executive Orders are Controversial

Executive Orders are controversial because they allow the President to make major decisions, even law, without the consent of Congress. This, of course, runs against the general logic of the Constitution -- that no one should have power to act unilaterally. Nevertheless, Congress often gives the President considerable leeway in implementing and administering federal law and programs. Sometimes, Congress cannot agree exactly how to implement a law or program. In effect, this leaves the decision to the federal agencies involved and the President that stands at their head. When Congress fails to spell out in detail how a law is to be executed, it leaves the door open for the President to provide those details in the form of Executive Orders.

Congressional Recourse

If Congress does not like what the executive branch is doing, it has two main options. First, it may rewrite or amend a previous law, or spell it out in greater detail how the Executive Branch must act. Of course, the President has the right to veto the bill if he disagrees with it, so, in practice, a 2/3 majority if often required to override an Executive Order.

Congress is less likely to challenge EOs that deal with foreign policy, national defense, or the implementation and negotiation of treaties, as these are powers granted largely to the President by the Constitution. As the Commander-in-Chief of the armed forces, the President is also considered the nation's "Chief Diplomat." In fact, given national security concerns, some defense or security related EOs (often called National Security Directives or Presidential Decision Directives) are not made public.

In addition to congressional recourse, Executive Orders can be challenged in court, usually on the grounds that the Order deviates from "congressional intent" or exceeds the President's constitutional powers. In one such notable instance, President Harry Truman, was rebuked by the Supreme Court for overstepping the bounds of presidential authority. After World War II, Truman seized control of steel mills across the nation in an effort to settle labour disputes. In response to a challenge of this action, the Supreme Court ruled that the seizure was unconstitutional and exceeded presidential powers because neither the Constitution or any statute authorized the President to seize private businesses to settle labour disputes. For the most part, however, the Court has been fairly tolerant of wide range of executive actions.

The difference between executive order and an executive action?

An executive action is a broader term, describing all types of unilateral moves by a president. That can include executive orders, but it also includes proclamations, memorandums, and proposals.
Executive actions carry varying legal weight. Directives and memorandums — used to inform federal agencies of administration policy — do carry the same legal effect as an executive order, according to a Justice Department statement from 2009.
The actions are often controversial. Since the Constitution doesn't spell out any specific terms for how and when they can be used, executive actions are ripe for legal challenges.

Presidential proclamation According to political science professor Phillip J. Cooper, a presidential proclamation "states a condition, declares a law and requires obedience, recognizes an event or triggers the implementation of a law (by recognizing that the circumstances in law have been realized)". Presidents define situations or conditions on situations that become legal or economic truth. These orders carry the same force of law as executive orders—the difference between the two is that executive orders are aimed at those inside government while proclamations are aimed at those outside government.

The administrative weight of these proclamations is upheld because they are often specifically authorized by congressional statute, making them "delegated unilateral powers." Presidential proclamations are often dismissed as a practical presidential tool for policy making because of the perception of proclamations as largely ceremonial or symbolic in nature. However, the legal weight of presidential proclamations suggests their importance to presidential governance.

Presidential memorandum is a type of executive action issued by the **president of the United States** to manage and govern the actions, practices, and policies of the various departments and agencies found under the **executive branch** of the **United States government**. It has the force of law and is usually used to delegate tasks, direct specific government agencies to do something, or to start a regulatory process. There are three types of presidential memorandums: presidential determination or presidential finding, memorandum of disapproval, and hortatory memorandum.

Presidential Directives, better known as **Presidential Decision Directives** (or **PDDs**), are a form of an **executive order** issued by the **President of the United States** with the advice and analysis of the **National Security Council**. The directives articulate the executive's **national security** policy and carry the "full force and effect of law".

EXECUTIVE OREDR NO 13769 (PROTECTING THE NATION FROM FOREIGN TERRORIST ENTRY INTO THE UNITED STATES) a.k.a TRUMP'S IMMIGRATION BAN

President Donald Trump on Friday 27th January 2017 banned nationals of seven Muslim-majority countries from entering the United States for at least the next 90 days by executive order.

The order bars all people hailing from Iraq, Syria, Iran, Libya, Somalia, Sudan and Yemen. Those countries were named in a 2016 law concerning immigration visas as "countries of concern."
The executive order also bans entry of those fleeing from war-torn Syria indefinitely.
Trump also has stopped the admission of all refugees to the United States for four months.
The order also calls for a review into suspending the Visa Interview Waiver Program, which allows travelers from 38 countries -- including close allies -- to renew travel authorizations without an in-person interview.
Here is the order in its entirety:

The full text of immigration travel's ban

By the authority vested in me as President by the Constitution and laws of the United States of America, including the Immigration and Nationality Act (INA), 8 U.S.C. 1101 et seq., and section 301 of title 3, United States Code, and to protect the American people from terrorist attacks by foreign nationals admitted to the United States, it is hereby ordered as follows:

Section 1. Purpose. The visa-issuance process plays a crucial role in detecting individuals with terrorist ties and stopping them from entering the United States. Perhaps in no instance was that more apparent than the terrorist attacks of September 11, 2001, when State Department policy prevented consular officers from properly scrutinizing the visa applications of several of the 19 foreign nationals who went on to murder nearly 3,000 Americans. And while the visa-issuance process was reviewed and amended after the September 11 attacks to better detect would-be terrorists from receiving visas, these measures did not stop attacks by foreign nationals who were admitted to the United States.

Numerous foreign-born individuals have been convicted or implicated in terrorism-related crimes since September 11, 2001, including foreign nationals who entered the United States after receiving visitor, student, or employment visas, or who entered through the United States refugee resettlement program. Deteriorating conditions in certain countries due to war, strife, disaster, and civil unrest increase the likelihood that terrorists will use any means possible to enter the United States. The United States must be vigilant during the visa-issuance process to ensure that those approved for admission do not intend to harm Americans and that they have no ties to terrorism.

In order to protect Americans, the United States must ensure that those admitted to this country do not bear hostile attitudes toward it and its founding principles. The United States cannot, and should not, admit those who do not support the Constitution, or those who would place violent ideologies over American law. In addition, the United States should not admit those who engage in acts of bigotry or hatred (including "honor" killings, other forms of violence against women, or the persecution of those who practice religions different from their own) or those who would oppress Americans of any race, gender, or sexual orientation.

Sec. 2. Policy. It is the policy of the United States to protect its citizens from foreign nationals who intend to commit terrorist attacks in the United States; and to prevent the admission of foreign nationals who intend to exploit United States immigration laws for malevolent purposes.

Sec. 3. Suspension of Issuance of Visas and Other Immigration Benefits to Nationals of Countries of Particular Concern.
(a) The Secretary of Homeland Security, in consultation with the Secretary of State and the Director of National Intelligence, shall immediately conduct a review to determine the information needed from any country to adjudicate any visa, admission, or other benefit under the INA (adjudications) in order to determine that the individual seeking the benefit is who the individual claims to be and is not a security or public-safety threat.

(b) The Secretary of Homeland Security, in consultation with the Secretary of State and the Director of National Intelligence, shall submit to the President a report on the results of the review described in subsection (a) of this section, including the Secretary of Homeland Security's determination of the information needed for adjudications and a list of countries that do not provide adequate information, within 30 days of the date of this order. The Secretary of Homeland Security shall provide a copy of the report to the Secretary of State and the Director of National Intelligence.

(c) To temporarily reduce investigative burdens on relevant agencies during the review period described in subsection (a) of this section, to ensure the proper review and maximum utilization of available resources for the screening of foreign nationals, and to ensure that adequate standards are established to prevent infiltration by foreign terrorists or criminals, pursuant to section 212(f) of the INA, 8 U.S.C. 1182(f), I hereby proclaim that the immigrant and nonimmigrant entry into the United States of aliens from countries referred to in section 217(a)(12) of the INA, 8 U.S.C. 1187(a)(12), would be detrimental to the interests of the United States, and I hereby suspend entry into the United States, as immigrants and nonimmigrants, of such persons for 90 days from the date of this order (excluding those foreign nationals traveling on diplomatic visas, North Atlantic Treaty Organization visas, C-2 visas for travel to the United Nations, and G-1, G-2, G-3, and G-4 visas).

(d) Immediately upon receipt of the report described in subsection (b) of this section regarding the information needed for adjudications, the Secretary of State shall request all foreign governments that do not supply such information to start providing such information regarding their nationals within 60 days of notification.

(e) After the 60-day period described in subsection (d) of this section expires, the Secretary of Homeland Security, in consultation with the Secretary of State, shall submit to the President a list of countries recommended for inclusion on a Presidential proclamation that would prohibit the entry of foreign nationals (excluding those foreign nationals traveling on diplomatic visas, North Atlantic Treaty Organization visas, C-2 visas for travel to the United Nations, and G-1, G-2, G-3, and G-4 visas) from countries that do not provide the information requested pursuant to subsection (d) of this section until compliance occurs.

(f) At any point after submitting the list described in subsection (e) of this section, the Secretary of State or the Secretary of Homeland Security may submit to the President the names of any additional countries recommended for similar treatment.

(g) Notwithstanding a suspension pursuant to subsection (c) of this section or pursuant to a Presidential proclamation described in subsection (e) of this section, the Secretaries of State and Homeland Security may, on a case-by-case basis, and when in the national interest, issue visas or other immigration benefits to nationals of countries for which visas and benefits are otherwise blocked.

(h) The Secretaries of State and Homeland Security shall submit to the President a joint report on the progress in implementing this order within 30 days of the date of this order, a second report within 60 days of the date of this order, a third report within 90 days of the date of this order, and a fourth report within 120 days of the date of this order.

Sec. 4. Implementing Uniform Screening Standards for All Immigration Programs. (a) The Secretary of State, the Secretary of Homeland Security, the Director of National Intelligence, and the Director of the Federal Bureau of Investigation shall implement a program, as part of the adjudication process for immigration benefits, to identify individuals seeking to enter the United States on a fraudulent basis with the intent to cause harm, or who are at risk of causing harm subsequent to their admission. This program will include the development of a uniform screening standard and procedure, such as in-person interviews; a database of identity documents proffered by applicants to ensure that duplicate documents are not used by multiple applicants; amended application forms that include questions aimed at identifying fraudulent answers and malicious intent; a mechanism to ensure that the applicant is who the applicant claims to be; a process to evaluate the applicant's likelihood of becoming a positively contributing member of society and the applicant's ability to make contributions to the national interest; and a mechanism to assess whether or not the applicant has the intent to commit criminal or terrorist acts after entering the United States.

(b) The Secretary of Homeland Security, in conjunction with the Secretary of State, the Director of National Intelligence, and the Director of the Federal Bureau of Investigation, shall submit to the President an initial report on the progress of this directive within 60 days of the date of this order, a second report within 100 days of the date of this order, and a third report within 200 days of the date of this order.

Sec. 5. Realignment of the U.S. Refugee Admissions Program for Fiscal Year 2017. (a) The Secretary of State shall suspend the U.S. Refugee Admissions Program (USRAP) for 120 days. During the 120-day period, the Secretary of State, in conjunction with the Secretary of Homeland Security and in consultation with the Director of National Intelligence, shall review the USRAP application and adjudication process to determine what additional procedures should be taken to ensure that those approved for refugee admission do not pose a threat to the security and welfare of the United States, and shall implement such additional procedures. Refugee applicants who are already in the USRAP process may be admitted upon the initiation and completion of these revised procedures. Upon the date that is 120 days after the date of this order, the Secretary of State shall resume USRAP admissions only for nationals of countries for which the Secretary of State, the Secretary of Homeland Security, and the Director of National Intelligence have jointly determined that such additional procedures are adequate to ensure the security and welfare of the United States.

(b) Upon the resumption of USRAP admissions, the Secretary of State, in consultation with the Secretary of Homeland Security, is further directed to make changes, to the extent permitted by law, to prioritize refugee claims made by individuals on the basis of religious-based persecution, provided that the religion of the individual is a minority religion in the individual's country of nationality. Where necessary and appropriate, the Secretaries of State and Homeland Security shall recommend legislation to the President that would assist with such prioritization.

(c) Pursuant to section 212(f) of the INA, 8 U.S.C. 1182(f), I hereby proclaim that the entry of nationals of Syria as refugees is detrimental to the interests of the United States and thus suspend any such entry until such time as I have determined that sufficient changes have been made to the USRAP to ensure that admission of Syrian refugees is consistent with the national interest.

(d) Pursuant to section 212(f) of the INA, 8 U.S.C. 1182(f), I hereby proclaim that the entry of more than 50,000 refugees in fiscal year 2017 would be detrimental to the interests of the United States, and thus suspend any such entry until such time as I determine that additional admissions would be in the national interest.

(e) Notwithstanding the temporary suspension imposed pursuant to subsection (a) of this section, the Secretaries of State and Homeland Security may jointly determine to admit individuals to the United States as refugees on a case-by-case basis, in their discretion, but only so long as they determine that the admission of such individuals as refugees is in the national interest -- including when the person is a religious minority in his country of nationality facing religious persecution, when admitting the person would enable the United States to conform its conduct to a preexisting international agreement, or when the person is already in transit and denying admission would cause undue hardship -- and it would not pose a risk to the security or welfare of the United States.

(f) The Secretary of State shall submit to the President an initial report on the progress of the directive in subsection (b) of this section regarding prioritization of claims made by individuals on the basis of religious-based persecution within 100 days of the date of this order and shall submit a second report within 200 days of the date of this order.

(g) It is the policy of the executive branch that, to the extent permitted by law and as practicable, State and local jurisdictions be granted a role in the process of determining the placement or settlement in their jurisdictions of aliens eligible to be admitted to the United States as refugees. To that end, the Secretary of Homeland Security shall examine existing law to determine the extent to which, consistent with applicable law, State and local jurisdictions may have greater involvement in the process of determining the placement or resettlement of refugees in their jurisdictions, and shall devise a proposal to lawfully promote such involvement.

Sec. 6. Rescission of Exercise of Authority Relating to the Terrorism Grounds of Inadmissibility. The Secretaries of State and Homeland Security shall, in consultation with the Attorney General, consider rescinding the exercises of authority in section 212 of the INA, 8 U.S.C. 1182, relating to the terrorism grounds of inadmissibility, as well as any related implementing memoranda.

Sec. 7. Expedited Completion of the Biometric Entry-Exit Tracking System. (a) The Secretary of Homeland Security shall expedite the completion and implementation of a biometric entry-exit tracking system for all travelers to the United States, as recommended by the National Commission on Terrorist Attacks upon the United States.

(b) The Secretary of Homeland Security shall submit to the President periodic reports on the progress of the directive contained in subsection (a) of this section. The initial report shall be submitted within 100 days of the date of this order, a second report shall be submitted within 200 days of the date of this order, and a third report shall be submitted within 365 days of the date of this order. Further, the Secretary shall submit a report every 180 days thereafter until the system is fully deployed and operational.

Sec. 8. Visa Interview Security. (a) The Secretary of State shall immediately suspend the Visa Interview Waiver Program and ensure compliance with section 222 of the INA, 8 U.S.C. 1222, which requires that all individuals seeking a nonimmigrant visa undergo an in-person interview, subject to specific statutory exceptions.

(b) To the extent permitted by law and subject to the availability of appropriations, the Secretary of State shall immediately expand the Consular Fellows Program, including by substantially increasing the number of Fellows, lengthening or making permanent the period of service, and making language training at the Foreign Service Institute available to Fellows for assignment to posts outside of their area of core linguistic ability, to ensure that non-immigrant visa-interview wait times are not unduly affected.

Sec. 9. Visa Validity Reciprocity. The Secretary of State shall review all nonimmigrant visa reciprocity agreements to ensure that they are, with respect to each visa classification, truly reciprocal insofar as practicable with respect to validity period and fees, as required by sections 221(c) and 281 of the INA, 8 U.S.C. 1201(c) and 1351, and other treatment. If a country does not treat United States nationals seeking nonimmigrant visas in a reciprocal manner, the Secretary of State shall adjust the visa validity period, fee schedule, or other treatment to match the treatment of United States nationals by the foreign country, to the extent practicable.

Sec. 10. Transparency and Data Collection. (a) To be more transparent with the American people, and to more effectively implement policies and practices that serve the national interest, the Secretary of Homeland Security, in consultation with the Attorney General, shall, consistent with applicable law and national security, collect and make publicly available within 180 days, and every 180 days thereafter:

(i) information regarding the number of foreign nationals in the United States who have been charged with terrorism-related offenses while in the United States; convicted of terrorism-related offenses while in the United States; or removed from the United States based on terrorism-related activity, affiliation, or material support to a terrorism-related organization, or any other national security reasons since the date of this order or the last reporting period, whichever is later;

(ii) information regarding the number of foreign nationals in the United States who have been radicalized after entry into the United States and engaged in terrorism-related acts, or who have provided material support to terrorism-related organizations in countries that pose a threat to the United States, since the date of this order or the last reporting period, whichever is later; and

(iii) information regarding the number and types of acts of gender-based violence against women, including honor killings, in the United States by foreign nationals, since the date of this order or the last reporting period, whichever is later; and

(iv) Any other information relevant to public safety and security as determined by the Secretary of Homeland Security and the Attorney General, including information on the immigration status of foreign nationals charged with major offenses.

(b) The Secretary of State shall, within one year of the date of this order, provide a report on the estimated long-term costs of the USRAP at the Federal, State, and local levels.

Sec. 11. General Provisions. (a) Nothing in this order shall be construed to impair or otherwise affect:

(i) The authority granted by law to an executive department or agency, or the head thereof; or

(ii) The functions of the Director of the Office of Management and Budget relating to budgetary, administrative, or legislative proposals.

(b) This order shall be implemented consistent with applicable law and subject to the availability of appropriations.

(c) This order is not intended to, and does not, create any right or benefit, substantive or procedural, enforceable at law or in equity by any party against the United States, its departments, agencies, or entities, its officers, employees, or agents, or any other person.

DONALD J. TRUMP
THE WHITE HOUSE, January 27, 2017

WHAT TO KNOW ABOUT TRUMP'S VISA AND REFUGEE RESTRICTIONS

President Donald Trump's road to the White House was paved in part with hard-line promises such as building a "great, great wall" along the US-Mexico border and outright banning immigration from any nations "compromised by terrorism."

After a week in office, Trump has sought to make these dramatic steps the pillars of his national security policy, scrawling his signature on executive orders aimed at reshaping immigration across the United States.

Here's what you need to know about the latest controversial actions.
The text of the order doesn't name the countries, but a White House official said they are Iran, Iraq, Syria, Sudan, Libya, Yemen and Somalia.

The same order also suspends the US Refugee Admissions Program for 120 days until it is reinstated for nationals of countries that Trump's Cabinet believes can be properly vetted.
The total number of refugees admitted into the United States will be capped during the 2017 fiscal year at 50,000, down more than half from the current level of 110,000.
During his campaign, Trump vowed to ban Muslim immigrants from countries with a "proven history" of terrorism against the United States or its allies.
Friday's executive order gives the Department of Homeland Security leeway to prioritize refugee claims "on the basis of religious based persecution" as long as the person applying for refugee status is "a minority religion in the individual's country of nationality."
That would make it easier for Christians and other religious minorities in majority-Muslim countries to enter the United States than it would for Muslims in general.

Trump's order also cancels the Visa Interview Waiver Program, which once allowed repeat travelers to the United States to be able to forgo an in-person interview to renew their visa. Under the new order, these travelers must now have an in-person interview.
"We strongly believe that refugees should receive equal treatment for protection and assistance, and opportunities for resettlement, regardless of their religion, nationality or race," the International Organization for Migration and the U.N. refugee agency said in a joint statement.

How many people come to the US from countries Trump is targeting?

In the last fiscal year, 43% of refugees admitted into the United States came from the seven countries that could be affected by restrictions, according to data from the Refugee Processing Center.
The Obama administration had pushed to resettle at least 10,000 Syrian refugees in the United States as part of humanitarian efforts in 2016.
During fiscal 2016, which began October 2015 and ended September 2016, the United States admitted the following number of refugees from the seven countries: 9,880 from Iraq; 3,750 from Iran; 1 from Libya; 9,020 from Somalia; 12,587 from Syria; 1,458 from Sudan and 26 from Yemen.

Apart from refugees, there are also other types of visas issued by the United States. Here are the number of total US non-immigrant and immigrant visas issued to the **affected countries in** 2015: **15,509** to Iraq; **42,542** to Iran; **3,575** to Libya; **1,409** to Somalia; **11,962** to Syria; **2,153** to Sudan and **7,668** to Yemen.

CONSTITUTION BACKING

This contention is meritless, both constitutionally and as a matter of statutory law. Let's start with the Constitution, which vests all executive power in the president. Under the Constitution, as Thomas Jefferson wrote shortly after its adoption, "the transaction of business with foreign nations is Executive altogether. It belongs then to the head of that department, except as to such portions of it as are specifically submitted to the Senate. Exceptions are to be construed strictly." The rare exceptions Jefferson had in mind, obviously, were such matters as the approval of treaties, which Article II expressly vests in the Senate. There are also other textual bases for a congressional role in foreign affairs, such as Congress's power over international commerce, to declare war, and to establish the qualifications for the naturalization of citizens. That said, when Congress legislates in this realm, it must do so mindful of what the Supreme Court, in United States v. Curtiss-Wright (1936), famously described as "the very delicate, plenary and exclusive power of the President as the sole organ of the federal government in the field of international relations – a power which does not require as a basis for its exercise an act of Congress." In the international arena, then, if there is arguable conflict between a presidential policy and a congressional statute, the president's policy will take precedence in the absence of some clear constitutional commitment of the subject matter to legislative resolution. And quite apart from the president's presumptive supremacy in foreign affairs, we must also adhere to a settled doctrine of constitutional law: Where it is possible, congressional statutes should be construed in a manner that avoids constitutional conflicts. With that as background, let's consider the claimed conflict between the president's executive order and Congress's statute. Mr. Bier asserts that Trump may not suspend the issuance of visas to nationals of specific countries because the 1965 immigration act "banned all discrimination against immigrants on the basis of national origin." And, indeed, a section of that act, now codified in Section 1152(a) of Title 8, U.S. Code, states that (with exceptions not here relevant) "no person shall receive any preference or priority or be discriminated against in the issuance of an immigrant visa because of the person's race, sex, nationality, place of birth, or place of residence" (emphasis added). Even on its face, this provision is not as clearly in conflict with Trump's executive order as Bier suggests. As he correctly points out, the purpose of the anti-discrimination provision (signed by President Lyndon Johnson in 1965) was to end the racially and ethnically discriminatory "national origins" immigration practice that was skewed in favor of Western Europe. Trump's executive order, to the contrary, is in no way an effort to affect the racial or ethnic composition of the nation or its incoming immigrants. The directive is an effort to protect national security from a terrorist threat, which, as we shall see, Congress itself has found to have roots in specified Muslim-majority countries. Because of the national-security distinction between Trump's 2017 order and Congress's 1965 objective, it is not necessary to construe them as contradictory, and principles of constitutional interpretation counsel against doing so. Nevertheless, let's concede for argument's sake that there is conflict. At issue is a matter related to the conduct of foreign affairs – a matter of the highest order of importance since it involves foreign threats to national security. If there were a conflict here, the president's clear constitutional authority to protect the United States would take precedence over Congress's dubious authority to limit the president's denial of entry to foreign nationals. But there is no conflict. Federal immigration law also includes Section 1182(f), which states: "Whenever the President finds that the entry of any aliens or of any class of aliens into the United States would be detrimental to the interests of the United States, he may by proclamation, and for such period as he shall deem necessary, suspend the entry of all aliens or any class of aliens as immigrants or nonimmigrants, or impose on the entry of aliens any restrictions he may deem to be appropriate" (emphasis added). Section 1182(f) plainly and sweepingly authorizes the president to issue temporary bans on the entry of classes of aliens for national-security purposes. This is precisely what President Trump has done. In fact, in doing so, he expressly cites Section 1182(f), and his executive order tracks the language of the statute (finding the entry of aliens from these countries at this time "would be detrimental to the interests of the United States"). While Bier ignores the president's constitutional foreign-affairs authority (although Trump expressly relies on it in the first line of his executive order), he concedes that Trump is relying on a statute. He theorizes, nevertheless, that because Section 1182(f) was enacted in 1952, whereas the non-discrimination provision (Section 1152(a)) was enacted years afterward, the latter must be deemed to have amended the former – thus removing the president's authority to impose class restrictions based on the aliens' country of origin. Nice try. Put aside that Trump is principally relying on his inherent constitutional authority, and that the class restriction he has directed is based on national-security, not racial or ethnic considerations. Trump's executive order also expressly relies on an Obama-era provision of the immigration law, Section 1187(a)(12), which governs the Visa Waiver Program. This statute empowers the executive branch to waive the documentation requirements for certain aliens. In it, Congress itself expressly discriminates based on country of origin. Under this provision, Congress provides that an alien is eligible for the waiver only if he or she has not been present (a) in Iraq or Syria any time after March 1, 2011; (b) in any country whose government is designated by the State Department as "repeatedly provid[ing] support for acts of international terrorism"; or (c) in any country that has been designated by the Department of Homeland Security as a country "of concern." Trump is principally relying on his inherent constitutional authority. So, not only has Congress never repealed the president's sweeping statutory power to exclude classes of aliens from entry on national-security grounds; decades after the 1965 anti-discrimination provision touted by Bier, Congress expressly authorized discrimination on the basis of national origin when concerns over international terrorism are involved. Consequently, by Bier's own logic, the 1965 statute must be deemed amended by the much more recent statute. Bier concedes that, despite the 1965 anti-discrimination statute, President Jimmy Carter barred entry by Iranian nationals in 1980, after the Khomeini revolution led to the U.S.-hostage crisis. But he treats Carter's restriction based on national origin as an aberration. Instead, he insists, we should place more stock in the federal courts' affirmation of the 1965 anti-discrimination provision during the 1990s — specifically, in a litigation involving an alien from Vietnam who had fled to Hong Kong and objected to being required to return to Vietnam to apply for a visa when applicants from other countries faced no such requirement. But there is no inconsistency here. Bier perceives one only by overlooking the salient national-security distinction. The discriminatory treatment of Iranians was rationally rooted in anti-terrorism concerns, and was clearly proper. The discriminatory treatment of the Vietnamese alien was unrelated to national security or terrorism, and thus problematic. Trump, like Carter, is quite properly acting on national-security concerns. One can debate the policy wisdom of the executive order, which is plainly a temporary measure while a more comprehensive and thoughtfully tailored policy is developed. The seven countries the president has singled out are surely hotbeds of radical Islam; but he has omitted other countries – e.g., Saudi Arabia, home to 15 of the 19 suicide-hijackers who attacked our country on 9/11 – that are also cauldrons of jihadism. Furthermore, as I have argued, the real threat to be targeted is sharia-supremacist ideology, which is inherently hostile to the Constitution. Were we to focus our vetting, unapologetically, on that ideology (also known as "radical" or "political" Islam), it would be unnecessary to implement a categorical ban on Muslims or immigrants from majority-Muslim countries. That is critical because non-Islamist Muslims who can demonstrate loyalty to our constitutional principles should not be barred from admission; while Islamists, on the other hand, are not found only in Muslim-majority countries – other things being equal, a sharia supremacist from the banlieues of Paris poses as much of a threat as a sharia supremacist from Raqqa. Yet, all that can be debated as we go forward. For now, there is no doubt that the executive order temporarily banning entry from specified Muslim-majority countries is both well within President Trump's constitutional authority and consistent with statutory law.

WHERE THE IDEA CAME FROM

Moreover, contrary to common mythology, a multitude of studies have shown that Hispanics do not assimilate to American culture by the 3rd generation. Trump has studied the facts about Hispanic immigration to America and, the idea gave birth to this executive order (travel ban).

Facts about Hispanic immigration to America are often obscured by statistics about "immigrants". Such numbers are misleading, as not all American immigrants are Hispanic. To remedy this problem, the current post will look at various aspects of the Hispanic American population which are cause for concern.

As will be seen, Hispanic Americans are, in many measurable respects, more problematic than White non-Hispanic Americans. Because of this, increasing the proportion of our population which is Hispanic via immigration will damage America in many predictable ways.

A nation's government should only allow in immigrants if doing so is in the best interest of said nation's citizens. After all, these citizens are the people who pay for the government, and their ancestors were the people who created it, not to mention the national culture.

The only serious benefit ever offered by immigration enthusiasts is that immigration helps the economy. However, as reviewed below, the economic benefits of Hispanic immigration to natives don't even come close to making up for the relevant costs. Given this, it is in the national interest to stop the current wave of Hispanic immigration into the United States.

1. Welfare use

Hispanics use welfare more than Whites do. This is true when comparing immigrant Hispanics to immigrant Whites and Native Hispanics to Native Whites. Below, you can see the result of an analysis carried out by the Center For Immigration Studies which looked at welfare use by immigration status and ethnicity for the years 2009-2012. In every year, Hispanics had a higher welfare use rate than Whites .It is also noteworthy that poor Hispanics use welfare more often than poor Whites do. A similar result was found by the New Century Foundation when looking at data from 2004-2005:

Some critics of the above studies argue that Hispanics have larger households on average than Whites do. Given this, it may be misleading to compare welfare usage by household.

I don't think it is obvious which measure is better. Sure, Hispanics have larger families, but it is still likely that everyone in a household often benefits when one person in the family goes on welfare.

That being said, even if you look at individuals Hispanics still use welfare more often than Whites:

2. Crime

Normally, the first place to look for crime rates broken down by ethnicity is the FBI's uniform crime report (UCR). However, their racial categories only include Blacks, Whites, and Asians. For the most part, Hispanics will be lumped in with Whites and to a lesser extent with Blacks. The UCR also includes a Hispanics vs Non-Hispanic category scheme, but in that case Whites are lumped in with Blacks. Given this, the UCR is not very useful for comparing the arrest rates of Hispanics and non-Hispanic Whites.

Luckily, many large cities, such as New York and Chicago, and some states, such as California, do record arrest rates in a way that differentiates non Hispanic Whites from Hispanics. The relevant data was compiled in a recent report published by the New Century Foundation. The results, as can be seen below, show that Hispanics have a much higher crime rate than non-Hispanic Whites.

Happily, the US incarceration data is better than its arrest data. The DOJ does a good job differentiating Whites and Hispanics in its prisoner population reports. As can be seen below, said report not only show that Hispanics have a higher crime rate than Whites, but show that this remains true even when only comparing young males of each ethnicity, thus falsifying the myth that Hispanic crime rates are caused by ethnic differences in median age and/or sex ratio.

3. Health

In some ways, Hispanics are actually healthier than Whites. Unfortunately, they are less healthy in the ways that impact others: STDs and obesity rates.

According to the CDC:

> "In 2010, the gonorrhea rate among Hispanics was 49.9 cases per 100,000 population, which was 2.2 times the rate among whites."

> "In 2010, the Chlamydia rate among Hispanics was 369.6 cases per 100,000 population… nearly three times the rate among whites."

> "The 2010 rate of P&S syphilis for Hispanics was 2.2 times the rate for whites."

4. Education

Relative to non-Hispanic Whites, Hispanics don't do very well in school. Moreover, this has been true for decades, and the gap, which is present from an early age, is, at best, closing at a snail's pace.

5. Sexual Behavior

Hispanics are also more likely than Whites to engage in degenerate sexual behavior. This can be seen by looking at divorce rates, abortion rates, non-marital birth rates, and teen pregnancy rates.

Contrary to the assimilation myth, the proportion of Hispanic children being raised by a single parent is actually higher among native born Hispanics than it is among 1st generation immigrants:

6. Socio-Economic Status

Speaking of the assimilation myth, below we can see that even 3rd generation Hispanics have higher than average rates of poverty and welfare use and lower than average levels of educational attainment, home ownership, income, and insurance coverage.

7. Politics

Hispanics also differ markedly from White Americans in their voting patterns. Specifically, as reviewed in this article, Hispanics vote democrat in every presidential election whereas Whites vote republican. And no, Hispanics are not "natural conservatives". As is covered in more depth here, Hispanics hold liberal views on a wide variety of issues. And no, Hispanics do not assimilate into White culture and become as conservative as Whites, or even the mean American, with time. On economic issues, some assimilation takes place, but there is no data to suggest that it they totally assimilate. On social issues, if anything, Hispanics get more liberal as the longer they've been in the US.

"In evaluating their social values, first-generation Latinos are more likely to express views generally considered more conservative than second-generation Latinos. When asked whether they thought divorce was unacceptable, nearly half (46%) of first-generation Latinos reported they believe it is unacceptable, compared to three in ten (30%) second-generation Latinos. When asked about abortion, more than eight in ten (83%) first-generation Latinos said it is unacceptable, compared to about two-thirds (64%) of second-generation Latinos." – Pew (2004)

In fact, according to a 2014 study by Pew, 62% of foreign born Hispanics and 63% of native born Hispanics identity as democrat or lean democrat.

Some people think that the GOP can convert Hispanics into Republican voters by adopting the leftist worldview on immigration. Given what we have already seen, it should be obvious that this is false. After all, Hispanics disagree with Republicans on far more than just immigration, and even republican presidents who granted mass amnesty, such as Reagan, still lost the Hispanic vote.

Even stronger evidence was provided by an analysis carried out by the Center for Immigration Studies. This report looked at whether more pro-immigration Republican members of congress, as measured by their Numbers USA grade, received a greater share of the Hispanic vote than anti-immigration republicans.

As can be seen, being pro immigration (as signified by a low grade) did not induce more Hispanics to vote Republican. It was, however, associated with a fall in the proportion of non-Hispanic White votes the Republican received.

To put this into more concrete terms, consider another study done by the Center for Immigration Studies which combined data on the US's 100 largest counties from 9 elections and found that, even after controlling for median income and the percent of the county that was black, a 1 point increase in the proportion of a county that was immigrant was associated with, on average, a .59 point drop in the proportion of that county that voted republican in the presidential election.

The implications of this data could not be clearer: Hispanic immigration means the end of American conservatism.

In fact, this has already happened to a degree. Consider this: if the Hispanic proportion of the electorate had not grown since 1980 Mitt Romney would have won the 2012 election even if there wasn't a single non white person that voted for him. Romney won 59% of the white vote and if Hispanics were still 2% of the electorate, as they were in 1980, whites would be 85% of the electorate which means the white vote alone would have given Romney 50.15% of the vote. If we add on Romney's share of the Hispanic and Black vote that number rises to 51.08% of the vote. On the other hand, if we project our current racial demographics back onto past elections we find, based on New York, that the Republicans would have only won one presidential election in the last 27 years.

8. Hispanic Identity

Another interesting feature of Hispanic Americans is that they are more likely to think of themselves as Hispanic (or Mexican) than they are to think of themselves as Americans. A pew study carried out in 2002 found that this was even true of 41% of 3rd generation Hispanic Americans. More recent Pew Polling finds that this is true of the plurality (49%) of 3rd generation Hispanic Americans! Many Hispanics also don't identify as a typical American: Thus, not only are Hispanics different from Americans in a wide variety of ways, Hispanics don't even identify as normal Americans either.

Combine this with the data reviewed in this article showing that ethnic diversity tends to make people get along less well, and it should be obvious that Hispanic immigration will increase American's levels of alienation and social strife.

9. The Economic "Benefits"

At this point we've seen most of the costs of Hispanic immigration. In response to this, liberals will often say that Hispanics improve the economy by doing crappy jobs for little money and thus lowering the price of goods and so increasing the amount of stuff Americans can buy. Thus, immigrants grow the economy.

According to the Harvard labor economist Geroge Borjas, immigrants (we are talking about immigrants now instead of Hispanics because I couldn't find good data on Hispanic immigrants alone) add 1.6 trillion dollars to the US economy each year. Of this, 98.7% is consumed by said immigrants. 2.2%, or $35,200,000,000, goes to natives. Dividing this by the roughly 300 million "native Americans" in the US and you get $117 per person.

As can be seen below, there are about 16 million immigrant households in the US. This implies that each household increases the incomes of natives by $35.2 billion divided by 16,211,763 immigrant households = $2,171. This number can be contrasted with the impact on the public deficit that an immigrant has each year compared to a non-immigrant. This is equal to the amount they pay in taxes minus the amount they consume in government services. An analysis of this was carried out by the Heritage Foundation. It found that the average household added $310 to the deficit each year compared to $4,344 for legal immigrants and $14,387 for illegal immigrants.

In other words, immigrants add thousands of dollars to the deficit each year relative to what non-immigrant Americans do, and this completely dwarfs any plausible increase in the real income of non-immigrant Americans thanks to immigrants.

TABLE 6

Government Benefits Received and Taxes Paid per Household, 2010 (Page 1 of 2)

NON-IMMIGRANT HOUSEHOLDS

ALL MONETARY FIGURES ARE DOLLARS PER HOUSEHOLD	Households Headed by Persons Without a High School Degree	Households Headed by Persons With a High School Degree	Households Headed by Individuals With Some College	Households Headed by Persons With a College Degree or More	All Households
Number of households	10,083,618	31,099,306	30,986,396	31,857,640	104,026,960
Percentage of households	9.7%	29.9%	29.8%	30.6%	100.0%
Government Benefits Received per Household					
Direct benefits	$16,461	$13,884	$10,454	$9,004	$11,617
Educational benefits	$4,930	$5,341	$6,897	$5,463	$5,802
Means-tested benefits	$19,150	$8,147	$6,091	$1,891	$6,685
Population-based services	$6,408	$6,740	$6,490	$8,333	$7,121
Total benefits and services	$46,949	$34,112	$29,931	$24,691	$31,226
Taxes Paid per Household					
Federal taxes paid	$5,387	$10,944	$14,762	$31,878	$17,954
State and local taxes paid	$5,509	$8,525	$9,447	$23,068	$12,961
Total taxes paid	$10,896	$19,469	$24,209	$54,945	$30,916
Fiscal deficit or surplus per household	–$36,053	–$14,642	–$5,722	$30,255	–$310

LAWFUL IMMIGRANT HOUSEHOLDS

ALL MONETARY FIGURES ARE DOLLARS PER HOUSEHOLD	Households Headed by Persons Without a High School Degree	Households Headed by Persons With a High School Degree	Households Headed by Individuals With Some College	Households Headed by Persons With a College Degree or More	All Households With Lawful Immigrant Heads
Number of households	2,558,106	3,015,088	2,561,737	4,631,877	12,766,808
Percentage of households	20.0%	23.6%	20.1%	36.3%	100.0%
Government Benefits Received per Household					
Direct benefits	$12,212	$10,639	$9,094	$7,204	$9,398
Educational benefits	$9,786	$8,748	$8,873	$7,213	$8,424
Means-tested benefits	$19,762	$10,093	$7,022	$3,549	$9,040
Population-based services	$8,439	$8,030	$7,487	$9,017	$8,361
Total benefits and services	$50,200	$37,511	$32,476	$26,982	$35,223
Taxes Paid per Household					
Federal taxes paid	$7,207	$10,897	$15,416	$30,897	$18,320
State and local taxes paid	$6,000	$8,287	$9,572	$20,614	$12,559
Total taxes paid	$13,207	$19,184	$24,988	$51,511	$30,879
Fiscal deficit or surplus per household	–$36,993	–$18,327	–$7,489	$24,529	–$4,344

SR 133 ● heritage.org

TABLE 6

Government Benefits Received and Taxes Paid per Household, 2010 (Page 2 of 2)

ALL MONETARY FIGURES ARE DOLLARS PER HOUSEHOLD	UNLAWFUL IMMIGRANT HOUSEHOLDS				
	Households Headed by Persons Without a High School Degree	Households Headed by Persons With a High School Degree	Households Headed by Individuals With Some College	Households Headed by Persons With a College Degree or More	All Households With Unlawful Immigrant Heads
Number of households	1,746,857	916,231	440,179	341,688	3,444,955
Percentage of households	51%	27%	13%	10%	100%
Government Benefits Received per Household					
Direct benefits	$45	$50	$47	$19	$44
Educational benefits	$15,514	$13,067	$10,501	$9,508	$13,627
Means-tested benefits	$6,235	$3,755	$2,006	$815	$4,497
Population-based services	$7,554	$6,033	$5,039	$4,783	$6,553
Total benefits and services	$29,348	$22,905	$17,593	$15,125	$24,721
Taxes Paid per Household					
Federal taxes paid	$4,284	$4,694	$6,160	$10,339	$5,233
State and local taxes paid	$4,579	$4,418	$4,869	$9,901	$5,101
Total taxes paid	$8,863	$9,111	$11,029	$20,240	$10,334
Fiscal deficit or surplus per household	-$20,485	-$13,794	-$6,564	$5,115	-$14,387

Note: The count of households includes households in the Current Population Survey and a small number of persons residing in nursing homes.
Source: Heritage Foundation calculations based on data from the U.S. Census Bureau, 2010 Current Population Survey. See Appendix tables for more information.

SR 133 · heritage.org

10. Conclusion

In conclusion, the supposed economic benefits of Hispanic immigration are illusory. By contrast, the economic, political, and social, costs are very real. America is harmed by Hispanic immigration, not helped, and for any government that puts America's interest first there is only one way to deal with Hispanic immigration: reverse it.

WHAT IMMIGRANTS NEED TO KNOW ABOUT TRUMP'S ORDER

Immigrants living in the US should check with an immigration lawyer before attempting to travel outside the country. Amid the confusion over **President Donald Trump's executive** order limiting immigration, immigrants -- those living in the United States and those wanting to travel here -- are understandably worried. Here are some things you need to know:

How do I know if it affects me?

For now, **President Trump's executive order** affects citizens of seven Muslim-majority countries.
They are: Iraq, Iran, Libya, Somalia, Sudan, Syria and Yemen. But the executive order also makes clear those seven countries are just a starting point for a likely broader ban that might include more countries.

What can I do to protect myself?

If you're a citizen of any of the countries listed above, do not travel outside the US at least for the next 90 days.
If **you have a green card** (that is, if you're a lawful permanent resident of the US), you should be fine. That's the latest from the White House, which has gone back and forth. First it said, the order would include green card holders. Then it said, their situation will be considered on a case-by-case basis. And now, it says, "**as far as green card holders moving forward, it doesn't affect them**."

What if I have an emergency and I have to travel?

If you absolutely HAVE to travel, please consult an immigration lawyer first.

What if I am already abroad and need to travel back to the US?

If you're a citizen of any of the countries listed above, you may have difficulty getting back into the US.
If you're a **lawful permanent resident of the US** from any of the countries above, get in touch with an immigration lawyer before flying back. Even though the White House's latest guidance is green card holders won't be affected, it's best to check.

What if I'm a naturalized US citizen?

If you're an American citizen, you should be fine -- even if you are from one of the targeted countries.

Can my relatives fly back with me if I'm a citizen?

Not if you're from one of the countries listed above. In that case, **your relatives may face difficulties** at immigration upon entering the US.

What if I have family or friends who were waiting to resettle to the US as refugees?

The executive order also halted the refugee program, at least for the next 120 days. This applies to all refugees, not just those from the seven countries above. In the case of Syria, the resettlement process has been halted indefinitely.

What else do I need to know?

Know your rights. The Immigration Defense Project **has prepared a flyer** that outlines how to lawfully interact with Immigration and Customs Enforcement agents if they come to your house.

Here's what the executive order does and doesn't do, the challenges to it, and how the Trump administration responded.

Who is not affected?

The executive order applies only to non-U.S. citizens, so anyone with U.S. citizenship—whether that person in natural-born or naturalized—is not affected. But, Reince Preibus, the White House chief of staff, **said** on NBC's MEET THE PRESS that Customs and Border Patrol (CBP) agents would have the "discretionary authority" to question U.S. citizens coming from the seven countries. CBP agents **have had that authority** even before Friday's executive order.

"I would suspect that if you're an American citizen travelling back and forth to Libya, you're likely to be subjected to further questioning when you come into an airport," he said.

Who is affected?

For 120 days, the order bars the entry of any refugee who is awaiting resettlement in the U.S. It also prohibits all Syrian refugees from entering the U.S. until further notice. Additionally, it bans the citizens of seven majority-

Muslim countries—Iraq, Iran, Syria, Somalia, Sudan, Libya, and Yemen—from entering the U.S. on any visa category.*

On Saturday this included individuals who are permanent residents of the U.S. (green-card holders) who were travelling overseas to visit family or for work—though a senior administration official said their applications would be considered on a case-by-case basis. The official also said green-card holders from those countries who are in the U.S. will have to meet with a consular officer before leaving the U.S.

News reports suggested the White House overruled the Department of Homeland Security's recommendations on excluding green-card holders from the executive orders. Preibus, on MEET THE PRESS, denied that, then appeared to suggest that the order won't affect permanent residents going forward, but when pressed appeared to contradict himself.

"We didn't overrule the Department of Homeland Security, as far as green-card holders moving forward, it doesn't affect them," he said. But when pressed by Chuck Todd, the show's host, on whether the order affected green-card holders, he replied: "Well, of course it does. If you're travelling back and forth, you're going to be subjected to further screening."

On Sunday evening, John Kelly, secretary of the Department of Homeland Security, offered more definitive guidance. "In applying the provisions of the president's executive order, I hereby deem the entry of lawful permanent residents to be in the national interest," he said in **a statement**. "Accordingly, absent the receipt of significant derogatory information indicating a serious threat to public safety and welfare, lawful permanent resident status will be a dispositive factor in our case-by-case determinations."

The order also targets individuals of those countries who hold dual citizenship with another country. For instance, an individual who holds both Iraqi and Canadian citizenships—though the U.K. foreign secretary **said** the U.S. had assured him it didn't apply to U.K. nationals.

It does not apply to individuals who hold U.S. citizenship along with citizenship of another country—though a CBP agent can presumably question such a person based on his or her discretion.

Why were those seven countries chosen?

Trump had made national security a centrepiece of his election campaign—at one point calling for a **"total and complete" ban** on all Muslims coming to the U.S. Although the executive order does not do that, Sean Spicer, the White House spokesman, **said** on ABC's THIS WEEK that the president "hit the ground running, had a flurry of activity, to do exactly what he said he was going to do."

Spicer noted that the seven counties put on the list were chosen by the Obama administration. Indeed, it has its roots in the **visa-waiver program**. The U.S. allows the citizens of more than 30 countries to visit for short stays without a visa under this program. But that visa waiver does not apply if a citizen of an eligible country has visited—with some exceptions—Iran, Iraq, Libya, Somalia, Sudan, Syria, or Yemen on or after March 1, 2011—under measures put in place by the Obama administration. Those individuals must apply for a visa at a U.S. consulate. These seven countries are listed under section 217(a)(12) of the INA, 8 U.S.C. 1187(a)(12) of the U.S. code, and it is this code that Trump's executive order cited while banning citizens of those nations.

What is the impact?

The number of permanent residents from these countries is relatively small. For instance, 1,016,518 green cards were issued in 2014. Of these, 19,153 went to Iraqis and 11,615 to Iranians, **according to** the Department of Homeland Security's data. These two countries make up the overwhelming majority of U.S. permanent residents from among the seven nations, which together have 500,000 permanent resident in the U.S., **according** to PROPUBLICA. But the seven nations, as I **reported** this week, also account for 40 percent of U.S. refugee intake.

Trump himself seemed to dismiss the impact, **tweeting** Monday: "Only 109 people out of 325,000 were detained and held for questioning."

Numbers, however, seldom tell the whole story. There have been **multiple reports** since the executive order was signed of people being prevented from boarding flights; refugees, who had gone through the years-long process before being approved to come to the U.S., **stranded** in third countries; of **Iraqis** who had worked for years with the U.S. military being denied entry; of **Iranian students** stuck overseas; of U.S. tech companies **recalling** its foreign workers because of the possible impact. And there have been protests against the order at airports across the country, including at New York's **JFK International Airport** and **Dulles Airport** outside Washington, D.C. , and the **Los Angeles International Airport** where lawyers, demonstrators, and the media descended to witness the order's impact.

Is this a Muslim ban?

Technically, no. The ban includes seven majority Muslim countries, but by no means are these states the most populous Muslim countries, nor are they among the top sources of Muslim immigration to the U.S., nor have they produced terrorists in the same numbers as other Muslim countries not on the list. Indeed, Muslims from Saudi Arabia, Egypt, Pakistan, and other countries can still visit the U.S.

Still, advocacy groups challenging the order say a Muslim ban is precisely what it amounts to. Indeed, they cited former the words New York City Mayor Rudy Giuliani's comments Saturday on Fox News. Giuliani said that Trump had asked for a "Muslim ban," but one that was done legally. He said he and a panel of experts "focused on, instead of religion, danger."

"The areas of the world that create danger for us, which is a factual basis, not a religious basis," he said. "Perfectly legal, perfectly sensible."

He went onto say the ban was "not based on religion."

"It's based on places where there are substantial evidences that people are sending terrorists into our country," he said.

"What we've seen here is stunning," David Leopold, a Cleveland-based immigration lawyer who is a past president of the American Immigration Lawyers Association, said on a conference call Saturday with reporters. "No president ever ever has used the authority and statute of the law to ban people based on their religion, ban people based on their nationality."

He said President Carter's ban on Iranians in 1980 after the Islamic revolution "barred certain classifications, not the whole country."

Is there legal action?

Yes. Judges in four cities—Alexandria, Virginia; Boston; New York; and Seattle—ruled against the detention of individuals at airports—in cases filed by the ACLU and others. The rulings appear to be limited to those people already at U.S. airports or in transit. They do not appear to say anything about the legality of the president's actions. DHS said it would comply with the orders—and some, but not all, of the people being detained at airports were allowed to leave.

The rulings were in response to legal challenges filed by the ACLU on behalf of two Iraqis who were detained at JFK Airport. The group also filed what's known as a motion for class certification, which would allow it to represent others who say they were detained at airports and other ports of entry to the U.S. But there may be challenges ahead.

Indeed, Trump has broad discretion under the law to bar a class of person deemed detrimental to the U.S. from entering the country. Leopold, the immigration lawyer, said the issue will have to be resolved by the courts."The problem we've got there," Leopold said, " is that this is unprecedented."

LEGAL BATTLE BEGIN
Judges temporarily block part of Trump's immigration order, White House stands by it

A federal judge in New York blocked part of President Donald Trump's controversial executive order on immigration, ruling that authorities could not remove individuals from seven Muslim-majority countries who had arrived in US airports after the order had been issued. The White House, however, maintained that the ruling does not undercut the executive order

US Judge Ann M. Donnelly held that the petitioners had a "strong likelihood of success" in establishing that their removal "violates their rights to Due Process and Equal Protection guaranteed by the United States Constitution."
Donnelly, who was appointed to the bench by President Barack Obama, sits on the US District Court for the Eastern District of New York.
A White House spokesperson defended the order, saying: "It is the right and duty of the President to do everything in his legal and constitutional power to protect the American people."
"Saturday's ruling does not undercut the President's executive order. All stopped visas will remain stopped. All halted admissions will remain halted. All restricted travel will remain prohibited. The executive order is a vital action toward strengthening America's borders, and therefore sovereignty. The order remains in place," the spokesperson said.
The court's ruling came after immigration lawyers at the Americans Civil Liberties Union and other groups flocked to airports across the country to come to the aide of individuals who had arrived with valid immigrant visas and found themselves in legal limbo. The lawyers asked for a nationwide stay that would block the deportation of all people stranded in US airports under what the group called "President Trump's new Muslim ban."

Donnelly granted their request, writing: "There is imminent danger that, absent the stay of removal, there will be substantial and irreparable injury to refugees, visa-holders, and other individuals from nations subject to the January 27, 2017, Executive Order."
Trump's order, titled "Protection Of The Nation From Foreign Terrorist Entry Into The United States," makes good on his longtime campaign promise to tighten borders and halt certain refugees from entering the United States.
As well as the ban on travel from seven named countries for 90 days, it also caps the total number of refugees admitted into the United States during the 2017 fiscal year at 50,000, down more than half from the current level of 110,000. It halts all refugees from Syria indefinitely.
"I am establishing new vetting measures to keep radical Islamic terrorists out of the United States of America," Trump said during the signing at the Pentagon. "We don't want them here."
As Donnelly was considering the case, lawyers around the country rushed to file legal briefs.

Early Sunday morning, a federal court in Massachusetts also issued a temporary restraining order, blocking part of the executive order in a case brought by lawyers for two lawful permanent residents who are college professors. That order, issued by United States District Court Judge Allison D. Burroughs, also an Obama appointee, went a step further ordering that the government could not "detain or remove" individuals who had arrived legally from the countries subject to Trump's order: Iraq, Syria, Iran, Sudan, Libya, Somalia and Yemen.

Burroughs said that her order applied to the petitioners in the case as well as those similarly situated including lawful permanent residents, citizens, visa-holders, approved refugees, and other individuals from nations who are subject to the January 27, 2017, executive order. The order was also signed by United States Magistrate Judge Gail Dein. The judges specified that the order would remain in effect for seven days while the court scheduled a hearing.

Lawsuit success

The United States denied entry to 109 travelers heading to the country at the time the ruling was signed, a Department of Homeland Security official said. The agency would not say how many of the 109 were sent already home and how many were detained.

The ruling does not necessarily mean the people being held at airports across the US are going to be released, said Zachary Manfredi, from Yale's Worker and Immigrant Rights Advocacy Clinic, who helped draft the emergency stay motion.

"The judge's order is that they (lawful visa/green card holders) not be removed from the US -- it doesn't immediately order that they be released from detention," he told CNN.

"We are hoping that (Customs and Border Patrol), now that they no longer have a reason to detain them, will release them. But it is also possible they could be transferred to (other) detention facilities," Manfredi said.

"We are getting the order to as many (Customs and Border Patrol) officers as possible right now," he added.

ACLU officials praised the judge's ruling.

Trump's immigration order: Which countries are affected?

"Clearly the judge understood the possibility for irreparable harm to hundreds of immigrants and lawful visitors to this country," said ACLU executive director Anthony D. Romero. "Our courts today worked as they should as bulwarks against government abuse or unconstitutional policies and orders. On week one, Donald Trump suffered his first loss in court."

Lee Gelernt, deputy director of the ACLU's Immigrants' Rights Project, who argued the case, said the ruling "preserves the status quo and ensures that people who have been granted permission to be in this country are not illegally removed off US soil."

Lawsuit is first challenge to executive order

The class-action lawsuit in New York is the first legal challenge to Trump's controversial executive order, which indefinitely suspends admissions for Syrian refugees and limits the flow of other refugees into the United States by instituting what the President has called "extreme vetting" of immigrants.

The two Iraqis, Hameed Khalid Darweesh and Haider Sameer Abdulkaleq Alshawi, had been released by Saturday night. But lawyers for other detained travelers said in a court filing that "dozens and dozens" of individuals remained held at JFK.

Similar legal actions were initiated in other states before the ruling in New York took effect.

A federal court in Washington State issued a stay forbidding travelers being detained there from being sent back to their home country.

A federal court in Virginia has issued a temporary restraining order saying several dozen permanent residents returning from trips abroad should have access to lawyers while they are being detained at Dulles International Airport and these residents cannot be removed from the United States for seven days.

'America is the land of freedom'

According to court papers, both Darweesh and Alshawi were legally allowed to come into the US but were detained in accordance with Trump's order.

Darweesh, who worked as an interpreter for the US during the Iraq War, was released from detention early Saturday afternoon.

"America is the land of freedom," he told reporters at the airport shortly after his release. "America is the greatest nation."

A source with knowledge of the case confirmed Darweesh will be allowed into the US due to provisions in Trump's order that allow the State and Homeland Security departments to admit individuals into the US on a case-by-case base for certain reasons, including when the person is already in transit and it would cause undue hardship and would not pose a threat to the security of the US.

The suit said Darweesh held a special immigrant visa, which he was granted the day of Trump's inauguration on January 20, due to his work for the US government from 2003 to 2013.

Alshawi was released on Saturday night, according to his attorney, Mark Doss.

Rep. Nydia Velazquez, D-New York, who had arrived at JFK by early Saturday afternoon to try and secure the release of the two Iraqis, railed against Trump's order and pledged continued action.

"This should not happen in America," Velazquez said following Darweesh's release. "One-by-one, street-by-street, if we have to go to court, we will fight this anyplace, anywhere."

'The executive order is unlawful'

The lawsuit said the US granted Alshawi a visa earlier this month to meet with his wife and son, whom the US already granted refugee status for her association with the US military.

The lawyers for the two men called for a hearing because they maintain the detention of people with valid visas is illegal.

"Because the executive order is unlawful as applied to petitioners, their continued detention based solely on the executive order violates their Fifth Amendment procedural and substantive due process rights," the lawyers argue in court papers.

Court papers said Customs and Border Patrol authorities did not allow the lawyers to meet with the men, and told them to try reaching Trump. Velázquez and fellow New York Democratic Rep. Jerrold Nadler said they attempted to speak to Darweesh and Alshawi at JFK's Terminal 4 earlier Saturday but were denied.

The ban and its impact

"When Mr. Darweesh's attorneys approached CBP requesting to speak with Mr. Darweesh, CBP indicated that they were not the ones to talk to about seeing their client. When the attorneys asked, 'Who is the person to talk to?' the CBP agents responded, 'Mr. President. Call Mr. Trump,' "the court papers read.

Doss, an attorney with the International Refugee Assistance Project, told CNN his clients knew they had to get to the US as soon as possible so they boarded the first flight they could.

The two men had been allowed to make phone calls. They do not know each other, and it is unclear if they were held together or separately, or if they were kept in a holding cell, according to Doss.

The lawsuit was earlier reported by The New York Times.

LEGALITY QUESTIONED

Trump immigration order: Families feel the impact
But the order immediately raised questions about its legal standing.

"What this order does is to take people who played by the rules that have been rigorously vetted and slams the door of the country in their face because of their religion," said David Leopold, an immigration attorney and the former president of the American Immigration Lawyers Association.

But Stephen Yale-Loehr, a professor of immigration law practice at Cornell Law School, said Trump's order may have merit.

"The plaintiffs are alleging a variety of reasons why they should not be detained under the executive order. Their arguments include the equal protection clause of the Constitution and a provision in the immigration law that prohibits national origin discrimination," Yale-Loehr said. "However, presidents have wide discretion on immigration, because immigration touches national sovereignty and foreign relations. Courts tend to defer to whatever a president declares on immigration. I think the administration could win."

An administration official told CNN if a person has a valid visa to enter the US but is a citizen of one of the seven countries under the temporary travel ban, then the person cannot come into the US. If the person landed after the order was signed Friday afternoon, then the person would be detained and put back on a flight to their country of citizenship.

Separately, Department of Homeland Security officials acknowledged people who were in the air would be detained upon arrival and put back on a plane to their home country. An official was not able to provide numbers of how many have already been detained.

Progressives outraged

Democrats and liberal-leaning groups continued to denounce Trump's order Saturday as racist.

"The first two refugees kept out of America by President Trump's order are Iraqis who helped US troops survive during the war," Rep. Jim Cooper, D-Tennessee, said on Twitter. "These men risked their lives for years to keep our troops safe. One was with the 101st Airborne. This is no way to treat our allies."

Vermont Sen. Bernie Sanders called the action an "anti-Muslim order" that "plays into the hands of fanatics wishing to harm America."

And Senate Minority Leader Chuck Schumer called on the Trump administration to "rescind these anti-American executive actions that will do absolutely nothing to improve our safety."

Travelers turned away

Sarah Assali from Allentown, Pennsylvania, told CNN that the US government stopped six of her Syrian family members at Philadelphia International Airport and sent them back to Doha, Qatar, the origin city of their flight.

Assali said her family members were persecuted Christians and did not speak very good English, so they did not fully understand why they were being put on a plane back to the Middle East.

Additionally, some US-bound travelers who were either refugees or from countries specified in Trump's executive ban have been turned back from Cairo International Airport, according to a Cairo airport official who is not authorized to speak to the media.

The official said they were required to follow the instructions of the United States in the matter. He said "(The airport personnel) have no choice but to follow orders. I don't want to blame anyone here."

US court refuses to reinstate Trump's Immigration ban

In setback to US president, appeals court declines to back ban on travellers from seven predominantly Muslim countries.

A federal appeals court refused to reinstate President Donald Trump's ban on travelers from seven predominantly Muslim nations, dealing another legal setback to the new administration's immigration policy.

In a unanimous decision, the panel of three judges from the San Francisco-based 9th U.S. Circuit Court of Appeals declined to block a lower-court ruling that suspended the ban and allowed previously barred travelers to enter the U.S. An appeal to the U.S. Supreme Court is possible.

The court rejected the administration's claim that it did not have the authority to review the president's executive order.

"There is no precedent to support this claimed unreviewability, which runs contrary to the fundamental structure of our constitutional democracy," the court said.

The judges noted that the states had raised serious allegations about religious discrimination.

Following news of the ruling, Trump tweeted, *"See you in court, the security of our nation is at stake!"*

Asked about Trump's tweet, Washington state Attorney General Bob Ferguson said: *"We have seen him in court twice, and we're two for two."* An appeal to the Supreme Court is possible.

Justice Department lawyers appealed to the 9th Circuit, arguing that the president has the constitutional power to restrict entry to the United States and that the courts cannot second-guess his determination that such a step was needed to prevent terrorism.

The states said Trump's travel ban harmed individuals, businesses and universities. Citing Trump's campaign promise to stop Muslims from entering the U.S., they said the ban unconstitutionally blocked entry to people based on religion.

Both sides faced tough questioning during an hour of arguments Tuesday conducted by phone — an unusual step — and broadcast live on cable networks, newspaper websites and social media. It attracted a huge audience.

The judges hammered away at the administration's claim that the ban was motivated by terrorism fears, but they also challenged the states' argument that it targeted Muslims.

"I have trouble understanding why we're supposed to infer religious animus when, in fact, the vast majority of Muslims would not be affected," Judge Richard Clifton, a George W. Bush nominee, asked an attorney representing Washington state and Minnesota.

Only 15 percent of the world's Muslims are affected by the executive order, the judge said, citing his own calculations.

"Has the government pointed to any evidence connecting these countries to terrorism?" Judge Michelle T. Friedland, who was appointed by President Barack Obama, asked the Justice Department attorney.

Rob Reynolds, reporting from San Francisco, said the court presented "a point-by-point rebuttal of the government's case in the ruling".

Speaking to media, Melanie Sloan, a consultant and a longtime ethics monitor in Washington DC, said: *"This tells the world that there is a significant portion of our country that is not behind this kind of thing at all. We will work very, very hard to defeat this kind of discriminatory ban that really doesn't help anybody." "I think you will see, going forward in the Trump administration, that often it will be lawyers and judges who will be on the forefront, stopping these abuses of power. Remember we are only in Week Three of the administration."*

'Thoughtful opinion'

Judge Robart temporarily halted the ban after determining that the states were likely to win the case and had shown that the ban would restrict travel by their residents, damage their public universities and reduce their tax base. Robart put the executive order on hold while the lawsuit works its way through the courts.

After that ruling, the State Department quickly said people from the seven countries — Iran, Iraq, Libya, Somalia, Sudan, Syria and Yemen — with valid visas could travel to the U.S. The decision led to tearful reunions at airports round the country.

Commenting on the 9th Circuit decision, Noah Purcell, Washington State's solicitor-general, described it as an "excellent, well-reasoned, careful, thoughtful opinion that seriously considered all the government's arguments - and rejected them".

He said it is *"important to recognize the real impact that this is already having on people's lives. We have just been hearing from people all over the state and all of the country about what a difference this has made, and we're so thrilled for that"*.

During his remarks at a law enforcement conference, Trump said the courts blocking his divisive immigration order "seem to be so political."

Trump's own Supreme Court pick, Neil Gorsuch, finds the president's comments about the judicial branch "disheartening" and "demoralizing," a spokeswoman for the nomination confirmation team told the media on Wednesday.

The Supreme Court has a vacancy, and there's no chance Gorsuch, will be confirmed in time to take part in any consideration of the ban.

The ban was set to expire in 90 days, meaning it could run its course before the court would take up the issue. The administration also could change the executive order, including changing its scope or duration.

"We could go on for several more rounds ... but presumably everything would be done very quickly, just as this has happened," David Levine, a law professor at the University of California's Hastings College in San Francisco, told Al Jazeera.

"The US government has several choices. One is that they could go to the Supreme Court in Washington ... to see if they can get a stay. The other thing they can do is try to and get a majority of judges in the 9th Circuit here to agree to review the ruling.

The government has 14 days to ask the 9th Circuit to have a larger panel of judges review the decision **"en banc,"** or appeal directly to the Supreme Court, which will likely determine the case's final outcome.

Section 2
People's Reactions

TRUMP TRAVEL BAN IS ANTI-MUSLIM FEAR-MONGERING, NEW LAWSUIT SAYS

WASHINGTON — The **Council on American-Islamic Relations filed a federal lawsui**t on behalf of more than 20 people that challenges President Donald Trump's immigration ban on Muslims as a First Amendment violation for singling out one religion that could lead to the expulsion of all Muslims living in the U.S. when their legal status expires.

Trump signed the executive order on Friday prohibiting Muslims from Iraq, Iran, Libya, Somalia, Sudan, Syria and Yemen from entering the U.S. A federal judge in Brooklyn issued the first injunction temporarily blocking implementation of the ban on Saturday. Judges in Virginia, Washington state, Texas and California followed suit.

"Five judges have had the opportunity to weigh on the constitutionality of this executive order, and we're batting five for five," said Gadeir Abbas, one of the attorneys who filed the suit. "Five have found constitutional problems with this executive order so we hope to put an end to it once and for all."

The Muslim advocacy organization's suit, filed in the U.S. District Court – Eastern District of Virginia, alleged that Trump's executive order violates the Establishment Clause of the First Amendment, which states that the government cannot endorse one religion over another. "The courts must do what President Trump will not -- ensure that our government refrains from segregating people based on their faith," said Gadeir Abbas, co-counsel on CAIR's lawsuit.

But, they forgot that the Immigration and Nationality Act grants broad-ranging powers to the President:

"Whenever the President finds that the entry of any aliens or of any class of aliens into the United States would be detrimental to the interests of the United States, he may by proclamation, and for such period as he shall deem necessary, suspend the entry of all aliens or any class of aliens as immigrants or non-immigrants, or impose on the entry of aliens any restrictions he may deem to be appropriate," part of the act reads.

This suggests Trump has a lot of leeway.

But another section of the law, which was passed in 1965 during the Civil Rights movement, states that "no person shall receive any preference or priority or be discriminated against in the issuance of an immigrant visa because of the person's race, sex, nationality, place of birth, or place of residence."

In an analysis piece, David Bier, an immigration policy analyst at the Cato Institute, wrote that such protection extends to green card holders and may not extend to non-immigrants such as refugees, asylum seekers, guest workers, tourists and temporary visitors.

CAIR said none of the more than 20 plaintiffs were detained over the weekend.

Another purpose of the executive order is "the mass expulsion of immigrant and non-immigrant Muslims lawfully residing in the United States by denying them the ability to renew their lawful status or receive immigration benefits," the lawsuit reads.

CAIR officials said they chose the federal court in a Virginia suburb close to D.C. because it is known for acting quickly.

"It takes two years for a Syrian refugee to come to the U.S. They are extremely vetted," said CAIR Executive Director Nihad Awad. "So eventually Donald Trump's executive order is not based on national security. It is based on fear mongering. He is still in the campaign mode."

Shereef Akeel, another CAIR attorney involved in the suit, said Trump's executive order sets a dangerous standard for extremist groups: If the U.S. prefers one religion over another, they can, too.

"That's giving them a gift," Akeel said.

A reporter who CAIR spokesman Ibrahim Hooper said worked for the far-right Breitbart News Network website was escorted out of the press conference announcing the suit.

"Breitbart and other hate sites often show up and we ask them to leave," Hooper said. "And each time they do they get some video and they post it online of how they're persecuted and that's just part of that game in Washington."

President Donald Trump's executive order **restricting citizens of seven Muslim-majority countries from travel to the U.S. is unconstitutional** because it creates "favoured and disfavoured groups based on their faith," according to a new lawsuit filed by the Committee on American-Islamic Relations in a Virginia federal court on Monday.

The suit against Trump, **Homeland Security Secretary John Kelly**, the Department of State, and the Director of National Intelligence names more than 20 plaintiffs, a dozen of whom are identified only as John or Jane Doe because of the precariousness of their legal position. It refers to Trump's order, officially known as "Protecting the Nation from Terrorist Attacks by Foreign Nationals," as the "Muslim Exclusion Order" throughout.

"Our First Amendment is under attack. We, as attorneys, are foot soldiers of the American Constitution and took an oath to protect all from being targeted by the government because of their faith," Shereef Akeel**,** an attorney who is co-counsel on the lawsuit, said in a press release.

The suit argues that Trump's executive order is both broader and narrower than the policy he proposed in December, when he promised "a total and complete shutdown of Muslims entering the United States until our country's representatives can figure out what's going on."

The executive order, the lawsuit argues, is narrower because it only applies to seven Muslim-majority countries. But it's also broader because it may interfere with immigration benefits for those who lawfully entered the United States from the seven countries on the list.

While the order "does not apply to all Muslims, the policy *only* applies to Muslims," the suit says.

Non-Muslims from the seven countries listed, including **at least one Yazidi Iraqi**, have also been affected by the ban. But the text of the order cites the perpetrators of the September 11th attacks as an inspiration for the ban (although none came from the seven countries affected), and Trump's allies have admitted it is an attempt to combat what they term "radical Islamic terrorism."

The plaintiffs list is a who's who of Muslim-American activists, including Arab American Association of New York Executive Director Linda Sarsour and Rashida Tlaib, one of the first Muslim women to be elected to a state legislature in the U.S.

But it's the stories of the anonymous plaintiffs that pack the emotional punch.

One is a Muslim American in Albany County, New York, who filed a marriage petition for his pregnant wife, a Sudanese national. Another is a permanent resident of Syrian origin whose citizenship application may be denied—even though he "is one of few critical care physicians servicing an underserved area in the United States," the lawsuit said.

"In the event he is prevented from returning to the United States, the area he serves will be lacking an essential physician to provide critical care to a substantial population in the United States," it states.

Another is a Syrian national who serves as an imam in Michigan. If he leaves the country, "he **will be prevented from returning to his home** and to his congregation despite his lawful permanent resident status, pursuant to the Muslim Exclusion Order, and based solely on his religious status as a Muslim and his Syrian national origin," the suit states. "Moreover, Plaintiff John Doe No. 1 will be denied citizenship in the United States, pursuant to the Muslim Exclusion Order, based solely on his religious status as a Muslim and his Syrian national origin."

Other anonymous plaintiffs include Somali and Yemeni student visa holders, a Syrian asylum-seeker whose ability to seek lawful permanent residency is now in jeopardy, a Sudanese national whose application for citizenship is being held up and whose Sudanese wife (though she has never lived in Sudan) is waiting to come to the U.S. through a marriage petition.

CAIR's lawsuit is not the first filed against Trump's executive order, but it is the broadest. Attorneys for two Iraqi men **filed** a class action suit in New York's Eastern District on Saturday, saying **detaining people with valid visas is unlawful.**

"Because the executive order is unlawful as applied to petitioners, their continued detention based solely on the executive order violates their Fifth Amendment procedural and substantive due process rights," they wrote.

Melanie Nezer, vice president for policy and advocacy at HIAS, a Jewish nonprofit, said Trump's actions could be devastating for refugees. "People will literally, if this goes through, not be allowed to get on planes, or arrive in the US and be told they have to go back," she said.
She said she wonders whether refugees who have already been approved for travel to the United States will have their papers revoked.
"So maybe they've given up their housing," Nezer said. "Maybe they're waiting at the airport and everything has been sold."
. They could conceivably be denied entry at airports or at the border."

PRECEDENT TO THIS BAN

Protestors rally during a demonstration against the Trump immigration ban at John F. Kennedy International Airport on January 28, 2017 in New York City. (Getty)

In the furor against President Donald Trump's ban on immigration, some are bringing up history.

Did President Barack Obama also ban refugees from Iraq?

Obama's administration did stop processing all applications for Iraqi refugees for a six-month time period. (Jimmy Carter and Chester Arthur were also among presidents to restrict immigration by nation state).

A 2013 ABC News article reported, "The State Department stopped processing Iraq refugees for six months in 2011, federal officials told ABC News – even for many who had heroically helped U.S. forces as interpreters and intelligence assets."

Trump's executive order stops all Iraqi citizens from temporarily entering the U.S. "on any visa category," affecting those trying to visit family or come here for work, in addition to live. It also affects six other countries. It originally included permanent legal residents of the U.S. with green cards, but on Sunday, the Department of Homeland Security said green card holders would be allowed into the country.

While Obama did halt the refugee program, it did not impact green card holders, or anyone with a visa. It also did not affect refugees who had already gone through the vetting process.

"Obama's policy did not prevent all citizens of that country, including green-card holders, from traveling the United States. Trump's policy is much more sweeping, though officials have appeared to pull back from barring permanent U.S. residents," the Washington Post reports. Trump's order gives preference to religious minority groups, such as Christians, when the admissions resume, according to The New York Times.

Obama didn't give any preference to religious minority groups, and his action was limited to refugee resettlement (certainly, it didn't affect green card holders, for example). However, Obama's pause in Iraqi refugee admittance had consequences for some people and was driven by a terrorism case involving refugees, ABC News reported. The network reported that, as a result of the pause, an "Iraqi who had aided American troops was assassinated before his refugee application could be processed, because of the immigration delays." (One of the first men detained under Trump's executive order, Hameed Darweesh, was an Iraqi interpreter for the U.S. military. He has now been released under an exemption in the order.)

Trump raised the Obama situation in a January 29 statement defending his immigration executive order. He wrote, "My policy is similar to what President Obama did in 2011 when he banned visas for refugees from Iraq for six months. The seven countries named in the executive order are the same countries previously identified by the Obama administration as sources of terror."

OTHERS DISPUTE TRUMP'S CONTENTION THAT HIS ORDER IS SIMILAR TO OBAMA'S.

"Why did Obama's administration stop processing the applications" suppose be a big question we all should have asked.

It stemmed from a case out of Bowling Green, Kentucky. According to the Associated Press, "Two Iraqi refugees plotted to send sniper rifles, Stinger missiles and money to al-Qaida operatives waging an insurgency back home against U.S. troops."

Waad Ramadan Alwan and Mohanad Shareef Hammadi were accused in the plot. ABC reported at the time, "Several dozen suspected terrorist bombmakers, including some believed to have targeted American troops, may have mistakenly been allowed to move to the United States as war refugees." Among them, said ABC, was Alwan: "The Iraqi had claimed to be a refugee who faced persecution back home" but his fingerprints were found on a piece of cordless phone wired to a bomb.

As a result, the government decided to check IED devices for fingerprints, according to ABC. More stringent vetting procedures were created. The Department of Justice press release announcing the two men had been sentenced quotes the U.S. Attorney as saying of them: "These are experienced terrorists who willingly and enthusiastically participated in what they believed were insurgent support operations designed to harm American soldiers in Iraq."

The Mirror describes what Obama did this way: "Paused approvals of refugee applications from Iraq for a period of six months after two Iraqi al-Qaeda terrorists were discovered living as refugees in Kentucky." The news site says Obama's action was in response to a "specific event" and designed to give authorities time to do the fingerprint matches off recovered IEDs.

According to National Review, President Obama also admitted very few Syrian refugees during his tenure.

There was some precedent for this. In 1980, according to Politifact, Jimmy Carter "ordered administration officials to 'invalidate all visas issued to Iranian citizens for future entry into the United States.'"

Here's specifically **what Carter said** in his address announcing those sanctions: "…the Secretary of Treasury [State] and the Attorney General will invalidate all visas issued to Iranian citizens for future entry into the United States, effective today. We will not reissue visas, nor will we issue new visas, except for compelling and proven humanitarian reasons or where the national interest of our own country requires. This directive will be interpreted very strictly."

Former U.S. President Jimmy Carter.

The Carter measure came in the height of tensions over the Iran hostage crisis. Carter also ordered Iranian students to report to U.S. immigration. Trump's order affects more countries but appears also tailored to nation states rather than the religious test he floated during the presidential campaign. However, because they are all Muslim majority and some minority religions are exempt from the ban, some are criticizing Trump for ordering what they are deeming a "Muslim ban." See the language in the order relating to that point here:

Trump denies that his order amounts to a Muslim ban, saying in a statement that 40 Muslim majority countries throughout the world are not affected by his executive order. He has argued that religious minority groups are singled out for persecution in the affected countries.

The courts will ultimately decide.

Pew Research noted that "after the 2001 terrorist attacks, the U.S. largely suspended refugee resettlement for about three months while security measures were examined."

As for **President Chester Arthur**, in 1882, he "signed the Chinese Exclusion Act, which stopped Chinese immigration for 10 years…The ban also prevented Chinese persons from becoming U.S. citizens, and the exclusion was subsequently extended permanently through later legislation," reported ABC News.

In 1917, during World War I, Congress passed legislation that barred "most Asian nation immigration overall, with the exception of Japan…and the Philippines," according to ABC News, which added that the U.S. only allowed 105 Chinese people to move to the country each year until 1965. In several immigration acts in the 1920s, reported ABC, the country established "a wide-scale quota system based on national origins."

Trump's immigration ban – which has been met by intense criticism and protests at airports throughout the country – temporarily stops immigration from six Muslim-majority countries: Iraq, Iran, Somalia, Sudan, Yemen, and Libya. The order also indefinitely stops immigration from Syria, stops all refugee resettlement for 120 days, and caps 2017 refugee admittance to 50,000.

A federal judge granted an emergency stay for part of the executive order on January 28, ruling that the government could not send back immigrants from the affected countries who are at airports being detained because they might suffer irreparable harm. A lawsuit has been filed asking the courts to deem the entire Trump executive order unconstitutional under the 5th Amendment, contending it subjects Muslims to disparate treatment. The Trump order has also affected people with green cards and those visiting America to see family or for work; there is a provision for case-by-case exemption in some circumstances. There have been reports of students, professors, and others stuck overseas or at airports who had lived in the United States for years. News reports said citizens of the affected countries were stopped from visiting relatives who live in America, and that Canadian citizens with dual nationality are also affected.

People attend an afternoon rally in Battery Park to protest U.S. President Donald Trump's new immigration policies on January 29, 2017 in New York City.

Obama signed the Visa Waiver Program Improvement and Terrorist Travel Prevention Act as part of an omnibus spending bill. The legislation restricted access to the Visa Waiver Program, which allows citizens from 38 countries who are visiting the United States for less than 90 days to enter without a visa."

National Review says that, before 2016, "when Obama dramatically ramped up refugee admissions, Trump's 50,000 stands roughly in between a typical year of refugee admissions in George W. Bush's two terms and a typical year in Obama's two terms."

The New York Times reports that about the same number of Christians and Muslims were admitted to the U.S. as refugees in 2016, despite Trump's claims that Christians had basically no chance to get asylum under President Obama.

A 2016 Fox News report found that Congressional data revealed "hundreds of terror plots have been stopped in the U.S. since 9/11 – mostly involving foreign-born suspects, including dozens of refugees." The report noted that some of those involved refugees from the affected countries, but other countries had more (Pakistan was top), and some terrorist suspects were born in America.

THE BAN'S CHRISTIAN FOCUS

President Donald Trump said in an interview that persecuted Christians will be given priority over other refugees seeking to enter the United States, saying they have been "horribly treated."

Speaking with the **Christian Broadcasting Network**, Trump said that it had been "impossible, or at least very tough" for Syrian Christians to enter the United States.

"If you were a Muslim you could come in, but if you were a Christian, it was almost impossible and the reason that was so unfair -- everybody was persecuted, in all fairness -- but they were chopping off the heads of everybody but more so the Christians. And I thought it was very, very unfair. So we are going to help them."

Trump did not name a reason or offer any evidence about why the agencies that vet refugees, including the Department of Homeland Security and the State Department, would have prioritized Muslim refugees over Christians.

According to a report by the non-partisan Pew Research Center, however, 99% of the nearly 12,600 Syrians granted refugee status last year were Muslims. Less than 1% were Christian. Syria's population is 87% Muslim and 10% Christian, according to the CIA World Fact Book.

Also on Friday, Trump signed an executive order explicitly freezing refugee applications from Syria. It's unclear how his pledge to help persecuted Christians from that country will accord with the order.

The United States admitted a record number of 38,901 Muslim refugees in 2016, according to a study conducted by **Pew**. But nearly the same numbers of Christians, 37,521 were also admitted.

At the same time, many Christian groups that resettle refugees in the United States decry the persecution of their brethren overseas, but said the country should not give favor to fellow Christians or bar Muslims.

"We would resist that strongly," Scott Arbeiter, president of World Relief, the humanitarian arm of the National Association of Evangelicals and one of nine agencies that partner with the federal government to resettle refugees.

"Some of the most vulnerable people in the world right now are Muslims. If we say no Muslim should be let in, we are denying the humanity and dignity of people made in the image of God."

Arbeiter said he and his group have tried unsuccessfully to meet with the new Trump administration to discuss refugee policy.

A study conducted by the libertarian Cato Institute found that between 1975-2015, the United States admitted approximately 700,000 asylum-seekers and 3.25 million refugees. Four asylum-seekers and 20 refugees later became terrorists and launched attacks on US soil.

"The chance of being murdered in a terrorist attack committed by an asylum-seeker was one in 2.73 billion a year," wrote the study's author, **Alex Nowrasteh.** *"The chance of being murdered in a terrorist attack committed by a refugee is one in 3.64 billion a year."*

Trump Defends Immigration Ban as 'Not About Religion. President claims visas will be issued again in 90 days as criticism mounts domestically and abroad.

President Donald Trump defended his travel ban of refugees and people from seven Muslim-majority nations and said the United States would resume issuing visas for all countries in the next 90 days as he faced rising criticism at home and abroad and new protests in U.S. cities.

Trump's critics have said his action violated U.S. law and the U.S. Constitution.

Outside the White House, where some viewing stands from Trump's Jan. 20 inaugural parade still stood, several thousand protesters denounced him, carrying signs such as **"Deport Trump"** and **"Fear is a terrible thing for a nation's soul."** Tens of thousands turned out at protests in cities and airports in New York, Los Angeles, Boston, Houston, Dallas and elsewhere.

Trump, a Republican, put a four-month hold on allowing refugees into the country, an indefinite ban on refugees from Syria and a three-month bar on citizens from Iran, Iraq, Libya, Somalia, Sudan, Syria and Yemen. Border and customs officials struggled to put Trump's directive into practice. Confusion persisted over details of implementation, in particular for the people who hold so-called green cards as lawful U.S. residents.

Senator Bob Corker, the Republican chairman of the U.S. Senate Foreign Relations committee and a Trump supporter, said the president's order had been poorly implemented, particularly for green card holders.

"The administration should immediately make appropriate revisions, and it is my hope that following a thorough review and implementation of security enhancements that many of these programs will be improved and reinstated," Corker said.

Trump defended his action. *"To be clear, this is not a Muslim ban, as the media is falsely reporting,"* Trump said. *"This is not about religion—this is about terror and keeping our country safe. There are over 40 different* countries worldwide that are majority Muslim that are not affected by this order."*

He added: *"We will again be issuing visas to all countries once we are sure we have reviewed and implemented the most secure policies over the next 90 days."*

WHITE HOUSE CHIEF OF STAFF REINCE PRIEBUS OPINION

white house chief of staff reince priebus said people from the seven countries who hold green cards would not be blocked from returning to the United States, as some had been following the directive.

"As far as green card holders moving forward, it doesn't affect them," Priebus said on the NBC program "Meet the Press."

Priebus added that these green card holders would be subjected to "more questioning" by U.S. Customs and Border Patrol agents when they try to re-enter the United States "until a better program is put in place over the next several months."

U.S. SENATORS JOHN MCCAIN AND LINDSEY GRAHAM OPINIONS

U.S. Senators John McCain and Lindsey Graham, prominent Republican foreign policy voices, said in a joint statement that Trump's order may do more to help recruit terrorists than improve U.S. security.

"Ultimately, we fear this executive order will become a self-inflicted wound in the fight against terrorism," they said, adding the United States should not stop green card holders "from returning to the country they call home."

"This executive order sends a signal, intended or not, that America does not want Muslims coming into our country," they added.

Trump blasted the two senators in a Twitter statement, calling them "sadly weak on immigration."

In another Twitter message, Trump said the United States needed "strong borders and extreme vetting, NOW."

"Christians in the Middle-East have been executed in large numbers. We cannot allow this horror to continue!" added Trump.

Trump's tweet did not mention that many more Muslims have been killed in the bloody Syrian civil war and other violence in the targeted countries.

Chuck Schumer, the top Democrat in the Republican-led U.S. Senate, seized on the mixed messages from Trump's administration after Priebus' comments.

"We need clarification. But it shows you, above the bad nature, the horrible nature of these (orders), the incompetence of this administration," Schumer told a news conference. "One hand doesn't know what the other is doing."

A senior administration official said green card holders would be subject to a rescreening but it had not been determined where and how those screenings would be carried out. Specific guidelines were being put together, the official said, adding: "They could be screened in many different ways and in many different places."

"I think banning refugees, banning immigrants, banning religions like Islam or any other religion, is un-American," said Will Turner, 42, draped in a U.S. flag among a crowd of several thousand people in front of the White House chanting: "No hate, no fear, refugees are welcome here."

MARK ZUCKERBERG RESPONDS ON TRUMP TRAVEL BAN

"My great grandparents came from Germany, Austria and Poland. Priscilla's parents were refugees from China and Vietnam. The United States is a nation of immigrants, and we should be proud of that.

Like many of you, I'm concerned about the impact of the recent executive orders signed by President Trump.

We need to keep this country safe, but we should do that by focusing on people who actually pose a threat. Expanding the focus of law enforcement beyond people who are real threats would make all Americans less safe by diverting resources, while millions of undocumented folks who don't pose a threat will live in fear of deportation.

We should also keep our doors open to refugees and those who need help. That's who we are. Had we turned away refugees a few decades ago, Priscilla's family wouldn't be here today.

That said, I was glad to hear President Trump say he's going to "work something out" for Dreamers -- immigrants who were brought to this country at a young age by their parents. Right now, 750,000 Dreamers benefit from the Deferred Action for Childhood Arrivals (DACA) program that allows them to live and work legally in the US. I hope the President and his team keep these protections in place, and over the next few weeks I'll be working with our team at FWD.US to find ways we can help.

I'm also glad the President believes our country should continue to benefit from *"people of great talent coming into the country."*

These issues are personal for me even beyond my family. A few years ago, I taught a class at a local middle school where some of my best students were undocumented. They are our future too. We are a nation of immigrants, and we all benefit when the best and brightest from around the world can live, work and contribute here. I hope we find the courage and compassion to bring people together and make this world a better place for everyone."

MALALA YOUSAFZAI

World-famous women's rights activist Malala Yousafzai's statement on President Trump's latest executive order on refugees:

"I am heartbroken that today President Trump is closing the door on children, mothers and fathers fleeing violence and war. I am heartbroken that America is turning its back on a proud history of welcoming refugees and immigrants — the people who helped build your country, ready to work hard in exchange for a fair chance at a new life.
I am heartbroken that Syrian refugee children, who have suffered through six years of war by no fault of their own, are singled-out for discrimination.
I am heartbroken for girls like my friend Zaynab, who fled wars in three countries — Somalia, Yemen and Egypt — before she was even 17. Two years ago she received a visa to come to the United States. She learned English, graduated high school and is now in college studying to be a human rights lawyer.
Zaynab was separated from her little sister when she fled unrest in Egypt. Today her hope of being reunited with her precious sister dims.
In this time of uncertainty and unrest around the world, I ask President Trump not to turn his back on the world's most defenseless children and families."

U.S SENATOR JOHN MCCAIN SAYS PRESIDENT TRUMP'S TRAVEL BAN WILL "GIVE ISIS SOME MORE PROPAGANDA"

Sen. John McCain criticized President Donald Trump's **ban on immigrants** from seven Muslim-majority countries, saying it has been a "confused process" that will only give the terror group ISIS "more propaganda."

"The good news is that it's only got to do with a pause," he told CBS' "Face the Nation. "The bad news is that obviously this process and these conclusions were not vetted."

McCain said that it's important to understand the "ramifications of this kind of action," which has been **roundly criticized by foreign leaders**.

"The effect will probably in some areas give ISIS some more propaganda," he said, adding that he is particularly concerned about the effect the ban will have on Iraqis -- whose troops are fighting side-by-side with American forces in the battle to retake Mosul.

He also blasted Mr. Trump for failing to consult with federal agencies or any foreign leaders before announcing such a sweeping action. As a result, he said, there's a great deal of "confusion" over the ban itself -- whether it applies to green-card holders, what happens to Iraqis who have been actively aiding the U.S. military, and other issues.

"There's so much confusion out there," he said. "And published reports are that neither the Department of Homeland Security or the Justice Department or others were consulted about this before this decision was made."

McCain said he is "worried" about Mr. Trump's changes to the National Security Council, which involved **adding his senior adviser Steve Bannon** to the group going forward.

"The appointment of Mr. Bannon is something which is a radical departure from any National Security Council in history," he said. "...And the role of the chairman of the Joint Chiefs of Staff has been diminished, I understand, with this reorganization. The one person who is indispensible would be the chairman of the Joint Chiefs of Staff, in my view."

He said he has no problem with Mr. Trump's **hour-long phone conversation** with Russian President Vladimir Putin on Saturday, but noted that U.S. leaders should never forget what Putin's real aims are.

"I think phone calls are fine -- I think that we have to understand Vladimir Putin for what he is," McCain said, citing Putin's annexation of Crimea, his bombing of hospitals in Aleppo and his attempts to "destabilize" other countries, including the U.S.

McCain, who was captured and tortured during the Vietnam War, said he hopes that Mr. Trump's selection of people like Defense Secretary James Mattis means the discussion about **bringing back waterboarding** and other enhanced interrogation techniques is over.

"I hope, I pray that it's done," he said. "I appreciate Gen. Mattis's comment, and especially Gen. Mattis's comment about what it does to the people who commit the torture -- that's an aspect of this that we probably haven't examined as much as we should.

GOP CRITICISM

"**GOP**" is a nickname for the Republican Party of the United States and stands for "Grand Old Party." The acronym reportedly dates all the way back to 1875, though the meaning has changed since its initial conception.
From their understanding, Trump has created the perception that he is banning Muslims from the United States.
Apart from McCain and Graham, here are voices of other Republican senators that criticized Trump so far.

"This was an extreme vetting program that wasn't properly vetted," Sen. Rob Portman, R-Ohio, **told CNN's Jake Tapper on "State of the Union."**
He said he's glad to see two federal judges temporarily block Trump's executive order, and said Congress should be involved in strengthening the nation's vetting of visa applicants.
"We ought to be part of it. We've been working on this," Portman said.

Sen. Ben Sasse, R-Nebraska, said in a statement that *"while not technically a Muslim ban, this order is too broad."*
"There are two ways to lose our generational battle against jihadism by losing touch with reality," he said. "The first is to keep pretending that jihadi terrorism has no connection to Islam or to certain countries. That's been a disaster. And here's the second way to fail: If we send a signal to the Middle East that the U.S. sees all Muslims as jihadis, the terrorist recruiters win by telling kids that America is banning Muslims and that this is America versus one religion."

Sen. Orrin Hatch, R-Utah, urged Trump's administration to tailor the executive order to be "as narrowly as possible."
Hatch said as a Mormon, he is aware that many of his ancestors were refugees himself, as he called on Trump to reduce "unnecessary burdens on the vast majority of visa-seekers that present a promise -- not a threat -- to our nation."

Sen. Jeff Flake, R-Arizona, like McCain and Graham, said Trump's executive order appears to target Muslims broadly.

"President Trump and his administration are right to be concerned about national security, but it's unacceptable when even legal permanent residents are being detained or turned away at airports and ports of entry," he said in a statement. "Enhancing long term national security requires that we have a clear-eyed view of radical Islamic terrorism without ascribing radical Islamic terrorist views to all Muslims."

Republican leaders silent

On ABC's T.V," Senate Majority Leader Mitch McConnell, R-Kentucky, said Trump should have "a lot of latitude" to secure the country by improving vetting of immigrants.

He said he opposes "religious tests," but did not specify whether Trump's executive order is one.

"The courts are going to determine whether this is too broad," McConnell said.

A spokeswoman for House Speaker Paul Ryan, R-Wisconsin, was similarly vague -- **telling The Washington Post**: "This is not a religious test and it is not a ban on people of any religion."

Democrats push back

Democrats from liberal havens to conservative states have equally condemned the travel ban.

Sen. Kamala Harris, a freshman Democrat from California, wrote to the Department of Homeland Security urging that Customs and Border Protection grant those detained at airports immediate access to lawyers.

Customs agents, she wrote, should "be directed to grant individuals detained at ports-of-entry throughout the United States timely and unfettered access to legal counsel."

And two red-state Democrats up for re-election in 2018 -- North Dakota Sen. Heidi Heitkamp and Montana Sen. Jon Tester -- both criticized the ban.

"This executive order is having harmful consequences on children and brave allies who are helping us fight terrorism," Tester said. "We must take strong steps to protect our nation from those who want to harm us, but we cannot sacrifice our religious freedom and our American values."

In **a lengthy Face book post**, Heitkamp wrote that Trump's move *"confirms the lie terrorists tell their recruits: that America is waging a war on Islam. This is outrageous."*

WHAT SOME OF CATHOLIC LEADERS SAID ABOUT TRUMP'S TRAVEL BAN

President Donald Trump, who won the majority of Catholic votes, is facing fierce opposition from Catholic bishops and non-profit leaders who are issuing strongly-worded statements condemning his executive order on refugees.

"We believe in assisting all those who are vulnerable and fleeing persecution, regardless of their religion," said Bishop Joe Vasquez of Austin, in a statement on behalf of the bishops after the order was issued.

Trump's actions have startled many Catholic leaders, said John Carr, a longtime policy director for the U.S. Conference of Catholic Bishops.

"It's so stunning, the scale of it, the immediacy of it, the bluntness of it," said Carr, who is now director of the Initiative on Catholic Social Thought and Public Life at Georgetown University. "This will remind people there were times when people who were Catholic were not welcome because of where they came from and what they believed."

The executive order blocks Syrian refugees from the United States indefinitely and prohibits admitting any refugees from other nations in the world for 120 days. For 90 days, no citizen of seven majority-Muslim countries will be admitted without a waiver.

The Catholic Church has a long history of helping refugees settle in the United States. Eighty-three Catholic dioceses out of 196 in the country are involved in resettling refugees in some way, according to a spokeswoman for the U.S. Conference of Catholic Bishops. Leaders of several Catholic agencies helping to resettle refugees denounced the order.

Catholic leaders point to the many remarks of Pope Francis in support of refugees. Francis said in the fall that people can't defend Christianity by being ***"against refugees and other religions,"*** noting that the sin Jesus condemns the most is hypocrisy.

"It's hypocrisy to call yourself a Christian and chase away a refugee or someone seeking help, someone who is hungry or thirsty, toss out someone who is in need of my help," he said when he met with Catholics and Lutherans in Germany in October. "If I say I am Christian, but do these things, I'm a hypocrite."

Some leaders characterized Trump's order as harking back to a time when Catholic immigrants from countries, such as Ireland and Italy, experienced discrimination, and when distrust of Catholics famously impacted President John F. Kennedy's 1960 campaign.

The historic tensions between Protestants and Catholics have faded since the 1980s, when socially conservative Catholics and evangelicals joined on causes, such as opposition to abortion and same-sex marriage.

Attitudes and political priorities have also shifted generationally, Carr said. He believes Catholics who voted for Trump 52 to 45 percent were motivated by promises Trump made to revive the economy and to appoint an anti-abortion Supreme Court justice.

The question of whether the United States works too hard or not hard enough for persecuted Christians overseas has been a widely debated question as conditions for religious minorities in the Middle East have deteriorated in recent years.

Under the Obama administration, some international religious freedom advocates say Christians and Yizidis who were targeted by the Islamic State were marginalized in key U.S.-supported United Nations' aid programs.

"Pope Francis was among the first to decry ISIS' genocide against religious minorities, so the fact that the executive order gives refugee priority to individual claims from persecuted religious minorities, whether Christian, Yizidi or Muslim, is welcome news," Nina Shea, who is Catholic and a senior fellow at the Hudson Institute, said in an email. ISIS is another name for the Islamic State.

The attitudes of Catholic voters on questions related to refugees tend to mirror those of the U.S. population as a whole. When asked in October whether the United States has a responsibility to accept Syrian refugees, 57 percent of Catholics said no, while 37 percent said yes, according to the Pew Research Center.

In an interview with CBN News, Trump said persecuted Christians would be given priority in applying for refugee status. But many Catholic leaders said that they are opposed to anything that would prioritize Christians over Muslim refugees.

"Any proposal that preferences Christians over Muslims as refugees makes Catholic leaders nervous because it feeds that narrative that this is a war between the Christian West and the Muslims," said the **Rev. Thomas Reese**, a Jesuit who sits on the U.S. Commission on International Religious Freedom – an independent government commission.

Bishops across the country expressed concern over Trump's executive order.

Cardinal Blase Cupich, Archbishop of Chicago, called Trump's order a *"dark moment in U.S. history." "We Catholics know that history well, for, like others, we have been on the other side of such decisions,"* he said in a statement.

When he was Archbishop of Indianapolis, Cardinal Joseph Tobin in 2015 defied then-Indiana Gov. Mike Pence, who is Trump's vice president, in settling Syrian refugees.

Tobin, now archbishop of Newark, issued a statement decrying Trump's order on withholding federal funds for sanctuary cities. He said such actions "do not show the United States to be an open and welcoming nation. They are the opposite of what it means to be an American."

On Monday 30th January, Bishop Michael F. Burbidge of Arlington, Va., released a statement calling for Catholics *to "to contact our elected officials to make our voices heard: our communities have been and will continue to be hospitable to refugees, in keeping with our legacy of welcoming the stranger."*

However, not all Catholic leaders were quick to condemn Trump.

Archbishop Charles Chaput of Philadelphia, who hosted Pope Francis' U.S. visit in 2015, denounced Trump's critics in a column published Friday 28th January around the March for Life. He suggested the University of Notre Dame should honour Trump with an honorary degree at graduation in the spring. Bestowing honorary degrees on presidents is a tradition for the university and caused a stir when the university issued one to President Barack Obama, given his positions on abortion.

"The archbishop will be writing about immigration and will probably touch on it, but he does not think it wise to engage in some of (the) frantic protests so far," Francis Maier, who is senior adviser to Chaput, wrote in an email. "This requires a reasoned response, not an anxiety attack."

Catholics are more likely than other Americans to be immigrants or children of immigrants, according to the Pew Research Center. The growth of the U.S. Church has been largely fuelled by Hispanic immigrants. According to 2014 Pew data, the share of U.S. Catholics who are Hispanic had grown by 5 percentage points since 2007 (from 29 percent to 34 percent), while the percentage of all U.S. adults who are Hispanic had grown by 3 points (from 12 percent to 15 percent). And the Hispanic share of Catholics is likely to continue to grow; among Catholic millennial, as many are Hispanic (46 percent) as are white (43 percent).

At St. Rose of Lima Catholic Church, an inner city parish in New Haven, Conn., where about 90 percent of parishioners are either immigrants or first-generation Americans, Trump's order produced alarm.

The parish hosted a "solidarity rally" on Tuesday 31st January 2017 that drew over 500 people from a variety of faiths and ethnic backgrounds, an event in which parishioners expressed empathy for Muslims particularly affected by the president's order.

The parish, which attracts 1,200 people on that day, is particularly sensitive to the risks facing immigrants: In 2007, 30 parishioners were deported during immigration raids in the city, according to the Rev. James Manship, pastor of the church.

"We've been frightened since the election – since the campaign, really," Manship said. "A nation has to have secure borders, but you can't treat people as a problem."

Some Catholic leaders have pointed out that the timing of Trump's Friday order coincided with the March for Life, which they interpret as a march for all lives, including those of refugees.

"Refugees and immigrants continue to believe that this nation is still a sanctuary, as they arrive with relief and thanksgiving. We pray they are never let down!" Cardinal Timothy Dolan of New York said at Mass the night before the march, according to The Atlantic. Dolan prayed at Trump's inauguration and praised his reinstatement of a policy blocking aid to foreign organizations that use funds from other sources to perform or discuss abortions.

Dolan told reporters he had not had time to review Trump's executive order yet. *"At first blush it causes us some apprehension,"* he said. He noted that the Catholic Church has been working on refugee issues since its inception *"because we are an immigrant church so don't be surprised that our strong bias is always in favour of the immigrants."*

WHAT WORLD LEADERS HAVE TO SAY ON DONALD TRUMP'S 'TRAVEL BAN'

European leaders, the United Nations and international groups have condemned **President Donald Trump's measures** against refugees and travellers from several Muslim-majority countries.

The **United Nations refugee agency** and the **International Organization for Migration** called on the Trump administration to continue offering asylum to people fleeing war and persecution, saying its resettlement programme was vital.

"The needs of refugees and migrants worldwide have never been greater and the US resettlement programme is one of the most important in the world," the two Geneva-based agencies said in a joint statement.

Germany and France also expressed discontent with Trump's measures.

"The reception of refugees fleeing the war, fleeing oppression, is part of our duties," **Jean-Marc Ayrault**, France's foreign minister, said during a joint news conference with his German counterpart, **Sigmar Gabriel**.

Germany has taken in more than one million refugees and migrants, mainly from the Middle East, since 2015.

Although traditionally open to asylum seekers, France has taken in far fewer refugees than Germany since the migrant crisis erupted.

Some in the French government, particularly ex-premier Manuel Valls, have criticised Berlin's open-door policy, as has Trump.

"The United States is a country where Christian traditions have an important meaning. Loving your neighbour is a major Christian value, and that includes helping people," said Germany's Gabriel.

"I think that is what unites us in the West, and I think that is what we want to make clear to the Americans."

Turkish Prime Minister **Binali Yildirim** also said the Republicans' sweeping ban on people seeking refuge in the US is no solution to problems.

"Regional issues cannot be solved by closing the doors on people," Yildirim said during a joint news conference in Ankara with Britain's Prime Minister **Theresa May**, adding that Western countries should do more to help ease Turkey's refugee burden.

May, however, refused to condemn Trump's refugee suspension.

"The United States is responsible for the United States' policy on refugees," she said when repeatedly pressed on the issue.

But other European leaders made their concerns clear, with Luxembourg Foreign Minister **Jean Asselborn** condemning the new measures.

"The decision is ... bad for Europe, because it's going to strengthen even further the mistrust and hatred towards the West in the heart of the Muslim world," he told the Sunday edition of German daily Tagesspiegel, excerpts of which were released a day in advance.

Inside the US, Democrats were also quick to condemn Trump's order, saying it would tarnish the reputation of the country.

"Today's executive order from President Trump is more about extreme xenophobia than extreme vetting," said Democratic Senator **Edward Markey** in a statement.

Chuck Schumer, the New York senator, also criticized Trump's move, saying in a tweet:

"There are tears running down the cheeks of the Statue of Liberty tonight."

Yet some Republicans praised Trump's move. **Bob Goodlatte**, chairman of the House of Representatives Judiciary Committee, said the US *president "is using the tools granted to him by Congress and the power granted by the Constitution to help keep America safe and ensure we know who is entering the United States"*.

"What we have to remember in all of this is that there are millions of Americans who like what Trump is doing when he's revamping immigration and the visiting to the US," Al Jazeera's Kimberly Halkett, reporting from Washington DC, said.

"It's what he promised to do during the campaign trail and in his **inauguration speech**."

Trump also ordered the **construction of a US-Mexican border wall**, a major promise during his election campaign, as part of a package of measures to curb undocumented immigration.

Ostensibly referring to Trump's executive order, Iranian President **Hassan Rouhani said** in a speech: *"Today is not the time to erect walls between nations. They have forgotten that the Berlin wall fell years ago."*

He added: *"Today is the time for peaceful co-existence, not the time to create distance among nations."*

But **Milos Zeman**, the president of the Czech Republic, praised the decision. Writing on Twitter, Zeman's spokesperson said Trump "protects his country" and called for the European Union to take similar measures.

Dutch politician **Geert Wilders**, known for promoting Islamophobia, tweeted: *"Well done @POTUS it's the only way to stay safe + free. I would do the same. Hope you'll add more Islamic countries like Saudi Arabia soon,"* using an acronym for the President of the United States.

UN EXPERTS SAY TRUMP TRAVEL BAN ILLEGAL, ENDANGERS REFUGEES

United Nations human rights experts are weighed in and they have expressed serious concern.

"Such an order is clearly discriminatory, based on one's nationality, and leads to increased stigmatization of Muslim communities," the experts said **in a statement to** REUTERS. In addition to placing an indefinite hold on refugees from Syria. Besides having a discriminatory effect, the experts say the order is illegal. Their statement says that the order *"risks people being returned, without proper individual assessments and asylum procedures, to places in which they risk being subjected to torture and other cruel, inhuman or degrading treatment."* They point out that sending refugees back to their countries goes against international law.

U.N. High Commissioner for Human Rights **Zeid Ra'ad al-Hussein** also said it's illegal to discriminate based on nationality.

One of the experts, **Nils Melzer,** the U.N. special rapporteur on torture, also said that he hopes that Trump doesn't use waterboarding or other methods of torture. While Trump has stated that he's personally in favour of torture, he has conceded that he will follow Secretary of Defense **James Mattis**, who says it doesn't work.

PROFESSIONAL NASCAR RACER DALE EARNHARDT JR. JUST PUBLICLY DENOUNCED PRESIDENT TRUMP'S TRAVEL BAN.

Eanhardt Jr, **who has been voted NASCAR's Most Popular Driver** a record number of 13 consecutive times, was expressing solidarity with a Muslim Twitter user named Gelar Budidarma when he made a statement about his own family's immigration history.

Kal Penn Just Blasted Trump Fans For Complaining About Celebrities: "You Just Elected One!

Actor and producer Kal Penn, who served in the Obama White House and on the Obama re-election campaign, gave an interview on CNN about a crowdfunding page he set up to raise money for Syrian refugees. Penn's efforts were a deliberate attempt to counteract the assumed tragic effects that President Donald Trump's recently instated Muslim ban will inevitably have on some of the world's most vulnerable populations.

Penn also had strong words for Trump supporters who are offended by celebrities speaking out against the new Administration. Their hypocrisy ought to be blatantly obvious given that they elected a celebrity to the highest office in America. When asked whether celebrity statements help or hurt the anti-Trump movement, Penn said,

"I DON'T KNOW. A REALITY TV CELEBRITY [TRUMP] JUST TWEETED ABOUT A SUPREME COURT PICK, SO I FEEL LIKE THAT CONVERSATION HAS SHIFTED SIGNIFICANTLY NOW THAT WE HAVE [A CELEBRITY] AS A PRESIDENT."

Just after the Muslim ban was implemented Penn, a native-born American citizen, received a hateful message online telling him that he did not belong in America. He told CNN, "What about the 14-year-old me or the kids who look like me who don't have the luxury of this kind of platform. Maybe we can raise $2,500 to show guys like that we're better than this."

His page quickly reached its goal of $2,500 and proceeded to raise OVER HALF A MILLION DOLLARS from donors in all 50 states and a total of 44 countries.. Penn continued on to give an insightful analysis of the Trump's ban.

"I think what the president is saying and doing is completely ridiculous. Who are the bad dudes miraculously coming in with ten hours' notice? Is it the army interpreters we detained over the weekend, the folks that saved American soldiers' lives? Are those the bad dudes? I find that insulting as an American citizen that you would infer that anybody who helped our soldiers stay alive are somehow 'bad dudes.'

"We have a vetting process in place America has been a place that welcomes people from around the world we do it safely we do it well. **NONE OF THESE COUNTRIES THAT ARE INVOLVED IN THE BAN WERE INVOLVED IN 9/11. EGYPT AND SAUDI ARABIA ARE NOT INCLUDED. JUST SO HAPPENS THAT THE PRESIDENT HAS PROPERTY INVESTMENTS IN BOTH THESE COUNTRIES.** *I mean you don't even have to read between the lines on how ridiculous this is."*

Penn's biting words are a powerful opposition to Trump's uninformed, bigoted policy making. More importantly, he backed up his sentiments with a commitment to doing something for refugees, people already in a dire situation that became much bleaker with one stroke of the President's pen. The resistance should listen to Penn and follow his example.

THE LAPD POLICE CHIEF OPENLY REBELLED AGAINST TRUMP'S IMMIGRATION ORDERS

Los Angeles Police Chief Charlie Beck told the LA Times that his department **will not be complying with President Trump's orders to assist the federal government in rounding up and deporting undocumented immigrants.**

"We couldn't deport 500,000 people if we wanted to, and if we did, it would be at the expense of public safety..." Beck said of the LAPD's resources. *"This is not our job, nor will I make it our job."*

Los Angeles has approximately 500,000 undocumented residents. Beck said in his experience, criminalizing these residents only makes for a more dangerous community.

"When you create a shadow population ... that fears any interaction (with police)," Beck said, *"then you create a whole population of victims, because they become prey for human predators that extort them or abuse them because they know they won't contact the police. Despite these policies which largely seek to demonize immigrant communities, criminologists largely agree that undocumented immigrants tend to commit less crime than natural-born citizens."*

Remember, during Beck's tenure as LA police chief, he has championed providing provisional driver's licenses for undocumented immigrants, arguing that the roads will be more secure if all drivers were regulated. He estimates that his force is approx. 47% Latino. Other city leaders have also pledged to risk their federal funding to defy Trump's immigration plans in San Francisco, Chicago, and New York.

"We have a very rich country with a lot of opportunity that is immediately adjacent to a poorer country with less opportunity," Beck said.

DAN RATHER WENT VIRAL RESPONDING TO TRUMP'S REFUGEE BAN

Legendary journalist Dan Rather **took to Facebook and pen a powerful condemnation** on this Ban and the ending of the refugee resettlement program:

"Today I shed a tear for the country I know and love, the one I believe still beats in the heart of most of its citizens.

The United States became the most powerful nation in the history of mankind not merely on the basis is its fearsome military, as lethal and well trained as th at m ay be. It w asn't solely based on it s u n preceden ted e con om ic en gin e, as dynamic and far-reaching as that may be. America's greatness was forged by a Constitutional compact of grand and universal ideals that the country has tried to live up to ever since.

For generations, we have been an imperfect but vital beacon of freedom to a world too often wandering and failing in moral confusion. But that ultimate strength has dimmed considerably in light of the recent actions on immigration from the new President Donald Trump. We are turning around desperate refugees. We are singling out men, women, and children on the basis of their faith – and we are doing all of this with a randomness and capriciousness that defies reason.

A colleague of mine used the term "heartless" to describe so much of the President's executive actions. Sadly, I found it an apt and dispiriting diagnosis—especially when faced with the results of his executive order on immigration. For over the years, I have seen that our greatest American leaders extol empathy rather than condemnation.

They have known that in a complicated world, it is best to make policy choices with a scalpel – not a hacksaw. Sometimes, when our national security is threatened at the level of World War II, all-out conflict is the only recourse. But those instances are by far the exception.

From Vietnam, to the Iraq War, from Japanese internment camps to the centuries-long persecution on the basis of race and ethnicity that almost toppled our democratic experiment, broad strokes channelling our least compassionate and most jingoistic impulses have always made us weaker rather than stronger.

Today, in the wake of his one-man decision to wreck and reverse immigration policy so suddenly, there is chaos and confusion mixed with heartbreak and fear. A well thought-out, measured overhaul of immigration policy, with organized-in-advance measures to implement that is one thing—and one that perhaps a majority of Americans would support.

But this mess, created overnight, is quite another. With this, we have emboldened our enemies who want to see nothing else than to compete in a world of moral relativism. In the Cold War, our struggles over civil rights fed into the propaganda of the Soviet Union – as our new actions fuel the extremism Mr. Trump claims to be attacking.

Too many people during the campaign explained away Mr. Trump's irresponsible rhetoric as metaphors and euphemisms. These are not concepts he understands. Serious foreign policy experts know that this is a boon for our enemies and undermines our democratic principles. But too many Republican leaders in Congress, even ones that denounced the Muslim ban during the campaign, stand by cheering it now. History will mark their names, as it marks this moment.

This will be challenged in the courts, who may very well strike it down. But damage, real damage, has been done to our global image. I believe Vladimir Putin is smiling, and would-be global powers like China see a vacuum forming that they will be eager to fill.

I still remain optimistic that the vast majority of American people will recoil and speak out at this unwise policy. But whether we like it or not, as the detentions and impediments already springing up make all too real, this is the stated de facto policy of the United States today. Every day that it goes on, every day the chaos, confusion and heartbreak deepens, America loses more pieces of its soul and standing in the world.

I desperately hope that the courts will fulfill their function and uphold the spirit of the Constitution in blocking the enforcement of these tyrannical edicts – which certainly violate the 1965 Immigration and Nationality Act, which precludes discrimination on the basis of national origin or place of residence.

But it is up to us, the responsible and concerned citizens of this once-great nation who are shocked and appalled at seeing our descent into the hellish abyss of fascism, to stand up and make our voices heard. It is extremely inspiring to see the thousands that are currently protesting outside of John F. Kennedy Airport **and** Chicago's O'Hare Airport. *That is exactly what Trump needs to see – the nation united in opposition to him and his heinous plots."*

THE ACLU SUED TRUMP

American Civil Liberties Union (ACLU) sued Trump on **behalf of two individuals impacted by the travel ban order**. The individuals in question, Hameed Khalid Darweesh and Haider Sameer Abdulkhaleq Alshawi are both citizens of Iraq and, were detained at the **John F. Kennedy International Airport** New York for no other reason than their nationality. According to ACLU both men have a legal right to enter the country.

The Director of the ACLU's Immigrants' Rights Project Omar Jadwat said in a statement:

"Our other plaintiff was also threatened because of perceived ties to the United States. President Trump's war on equality is already taking a terrible human toll. This ban cannot be allowed to continue."

According to the ACLU's lawsuit:

After conducting standard procedures of administrative processing and security checks, the federal government has deemed both Petitioners not to pose threats to the United States. Despite these findings and Petitioners 'valid entry documents, U.S. Customs and Border Protection ("CBP") blocked both Petitioners from exiting JFK Airport and detained Petitioners therein. No magistrate has determined that there is sufficient justification for the continued detention of either Petitioner. Instead, CBP is holding Petitioners at JFK Airports solely pursuant to an executive order issued on January 27, 2017.

"There was absolutely no reason to detain these men other than Trump's order which is highly discriminatory and unconstitutional," Omar Jadwat said.

ANGELINA JOLIE RESPONDED TO TRUMP'S TRAVEL BAN

World-famous actress and humanitarian activist Angelina Jolie has joined in condemning Donald Trump's ban on Muslims and refugees.

Jolie has a special perspective on this issue—all of her children were born abroad but are American citizens. From her statement, she points out that by banning refugees; we are turning away children and those who need us the most; branding them as unsafe though they are helpless, simply because of where they are born. Here are Jolie's words:

"I also want to know that refugee children who qualify for asylum will always have a chance to plead their case to a compassionate America. And that we can manage our security without writing off citizens of entire countries — even babies — as unsafe to visit our country by virtue of geography or religion."

"It is simply not true that our borders are overrun or that refugees are admitted to the United States without close scrutiny. "Refugees are in fact subject to the highest level of screening of any category of traveler to the United States. This includes months of interviews, and security checks carried out by the F.B.I., the National Counterterrorism Center, the Department of Homeland Security and the State Department," she adds.

Taking the step further, she makes an impassioned case for why refugees are not a threat to the United States, but are merely threatened themselves. Refugees flee brutal regimes and bloody civil wars, famines and droughts, floods and rising seas. **"Furthermore, only the most vulnerable people are put forward for resettlement in the first place: survivors of torture, and women and children at risk or who might not survive without urgent, specialized medical assistance. I have visited countless camps and cities where hundreds of thousands of refugees are barely surviving and every family has suffered,"** she added.

She reminds us that the US and the Western world barely accept a fraction of the world's refugees, in spite of being able to adequately house this population and provide them with some kind of opportunity. Jolie explains, **"And in fact only a minuscule fraction — less than 1 percent — of all refugees in the world are ever resettled in the United States or any other country. There are more than 65 million refugees and displaced people worldwide. Nine out of 10 refugees live in poor and middle-income countries, not in rich Western nations. There are 2.8 million Syrian refugees in Turkey alone. Only about 18,000 Syrians have been resettled in America since 2011."**

She reminds us that closing our doors to the refugees of the Syrian Civil War is condemning them to a death sentence as surely as it was to turn away the boats carrying Jewish refugees in the Second World War.

But more than that, closing our doors sends a message to Muslims around the world – and to Muslims living in the United States – that they are not welcome here. It makes the propaganda of extremist groups more effective.

"The lesson of the years we have spent fighting terrorism since Sept. 11 is that every time we depart from our values we worsen the very problem we are trying to contain. We must never allow our values to become the collateral damage of a search for greater security. Shutting our door to refugees or discriminating among them is not our way, and does not make us safer. Acting out of fear is not our way. Targeting the weakest does not show strength."

Angelina Jolie wants America to know that what Trump is doing is wrong. She could have been silent to not alienate any fans, but she spoke out, giving voice to those who cannot stand up for themselves—those who need advocates and support more than anyone, innocent refugees whose numbers are unfortunately growing by the day. These same refugees are in this situation *because* of the consequences of American aggression and now they are being denied even the hope of entry into America and a chance at a better life like our ancestors got.

DISNEY AND UBER'S CEOS QUIT TRUMP'S ECONOMIC PANEL

Public pressure was just too much for Uber CEO Travis Kalanick to bear. Kalanick was a late addition to President Trump's Strategic and Policy Forum, a circle of ultra wealthy advisors. Less than one week after President Donald Trump's Muslim ban immigration order was signed, the slogan #deleteUber protest campaign came to air.

Uber app users in the city and elsewhere started deleting Uber from their phones and spreading #deleteUber across Facebook, Twitter and other social media. On Wednesday being February 2nd, an association of Uber drivers **had petitioned Kalanick to cut his ties with Mr. Trump.**

"Earlier today I spoke briefly with the President about the immigration executive order and its issues for our community," Kalanick wrote in a letter obtained by The Mercury News. "I also let him know that I would not be able to participate on his economic council. Joining the group was not meant to be an endorsement of the President or his agenda but unfortunately it has been misinterpreted to be exactly that."

The CEO of the Walt Disney Corporation, Bob Iger, **also announced that he will be pulling out of Trump's economic council.**

MARK CUBAN BLASTED TRUMP'S "HALF-BAKED" TRAVEL BAN

Outspoken billionaire Mark Cuban slammed Donald Trump's management style and un-American Muslim ban on CNN. He believed that Trump's Muslim ban is causing real life misery all over America. A Syrian-born Doctor from Chicago **is suing for the right to return** home, and a family of Syrians **who voted for Trump** is now upset that the man they didn't take literally, literally tore their family apart with a single pen stroke. A **once-year-old burn victim is separated** from his parents while he awaits surgery; **another child who needs heart surgery will not be able to take advantage of American medical expertise.**

"Let's just be real, real clear. The ban was half-assed and half-baked, right? It was half-baked, it wasn't thought out, it was rushed, and it was ridiculous. When something like this happens, it calls in to question the management skills of the guy in charge."

Cuban continued with a great analogy about the security theater mindset which permeates the Trump regime's early moves, most of which he sees as pointless exercises of brute force:

"If the goal was security, why do you leave off any other countries that hosted terrorism? That's like locking your front door and leaving all of your windows open."

He went further and said that Trump's team wrote that the purpose of the irrational ban was alternative facts like 'keeping America safe" when all it does is put our nation more at risk.

"The reality is, we have an actual madman in the White House, and the Republican Congress is uninterested in acting as a co-equal branch of government and enforcing America's Constitution," Mark Cuban added.

"This man Trump is completely deranged, drunk with power and NOT ONE American official insisted he undergo a full psychiatric exam!! His father was strict and power-driven, superficial; his brother was scorned for just wanting to be a pilot and drank himself to death. Trump appealed to the rednecks; all packing guns, all still living in the 'confederate' age throughout his campaign. One can see how he struts with glee when working up a crowd, and now sits writing his signature, with flourish, on order after order without any communicative discussion neither with public nor press. He is uneducated in many things despite his 'now failed' real estate holdings, his speeches--lacking substance, and. lack of humility. .His sister is a judge.....reporters should seek her out for a 'family history' article."

Trump Has Already Been Sued 50 Times Since Taking Office

Following his inauguration, Donald J. Trump has been sued at a faster pace than any other president in history. President Trump has been the subject of at least 50 lawsuits during his first 11 days, **according to the New York Daily News,** and that number appears ready to grow.

The Citizens for Responsibility and Ethics in Washington is suing the president. The ACLU is suing the president. The Council on American-Islamic Relations is suing the president. Never before has there been so much legal action sought to oppose a U.S. president. For all the conservative consternation following Barack Obama's inauguration, he had only been sued 11 times at this point in his presidency.

Mr. Trump is no stranger to being sued. He was facing a **staggering 3,500 lawsuits before he even took office,** according to a USA Today analysis. The claims against the president range from fraud involving Trump University (there are three separate class actions) to breach of contract lawsuits filed by members of his golf club in Florida. These new suits are really just a continuation of Trump's trail of tears into the White House. It appears Mr. Trump can't go anywhere without attracting legal retribution. He was sued during his campaign for sending unsolicited text messages, urging a plaintiff in that case to "Make America Great Again!"

Airlines allow passengers after judge blocks travel ban

US Customs and Border Protection has informed major American airlines on a conference call that it was "back to business as usual," effective immediately, an airline executive told CNN.

The State Department has reversed the cancellation of visas provisionally revoked after Trump's executive order -- so long as those visas were not stamped or marked as canceled.

The State Department has said fewer than 60,000 visas were revoked since Trump signed the order January 27. It was not immediately clear how many from that group will continue to be without their visas because their visas were physically canceled.

Also, the Department of Homeland Security has suspended all actions to implement the order.

The department will resume inspections of travelers as it did before Trump's order, the agency's acting press secretary, Gillian Christensen, said in a statement.

James Robart

Emirates Airlines, Qatar Airways and Etihad Airways, major operators that connect the Middle East to the United States, said they would allow citizens of the affected nations on their US-bound flights. Emirates Airlines and Qatar Airways said those presenting a valid, unexpired visa or green card would also be allowed to board.

Air France also said it would accept passengers from the seven countries.

"Air France takes note of the decision of the American courts to suspend the presidential decree of 27 January 2017 prohibiting entry into the US for citizens of seven countries," the airline said.

"Consequently, and subject to satisfying the conditions of entry into the United States, as from today Air France will accept passengers from the countries concerned on its flights to the US."

Germany's largest carrier, Lufthansa, made a similar announcement but warned that "short-notice changes to the immigration regulations may occur at any time."

At New York's John F. Kennedy International Airport, an advocate for immigrants praised the judge's order and said her organization is trying to educate travelers and family members about the latest developments.

Camille Meckler of the **New York Immigration Coalition** said she expects arrivals to begin soon. She said it's a "terrible, terrible thing" that some visas were marked as canceled and that people will have to begin the long, expensive process of replacing them.

"We're going to continue to fight back," she said. "This is wrong. This isn't how you govern a country."

No rush to the US

The travel ban has caused confusion in many countries, raising questions of whether people with dual nationality would still be barred from entering the country.

It first appeared that the Trump administration would strike deals country by country, but the Department of Homeland Security later clarified that the ban did not apply to dual nationals with passports from countries not on the list.

People traveling on diplomatic, NATO or UN visas were also exempt from the ban.

Despite the judge's ruling and airlines' announcements that the ban was halted, there appeared to be no rush to the United States from the regional hubs connecting passengers from the Middle East.

Istanbul's Ataturk Airport was calm as flights departed as usual to Los Angeles, San Francisco, Atlanta, New York, Boston and Miami.

US District Judge James Robart, a George W. Bush appointee in Washington State, temporarily stopped Trump's travel ban 3rd February night.

The White House quickly responded, calling the order "outrageous" and vowing to appeal.

"At the earliest possible time, the Department of Justice intends to file an emergency stay of this outrageous order and defend the executive order of the President, which we believe is lawful and appropriate," White House press secretary Sean Spicer said in a statement.

The White House dropped the word "outrageous" minutes later in a second statement.

The political backlash for Trump has been equally severe, with the order driving numerous mass protests.

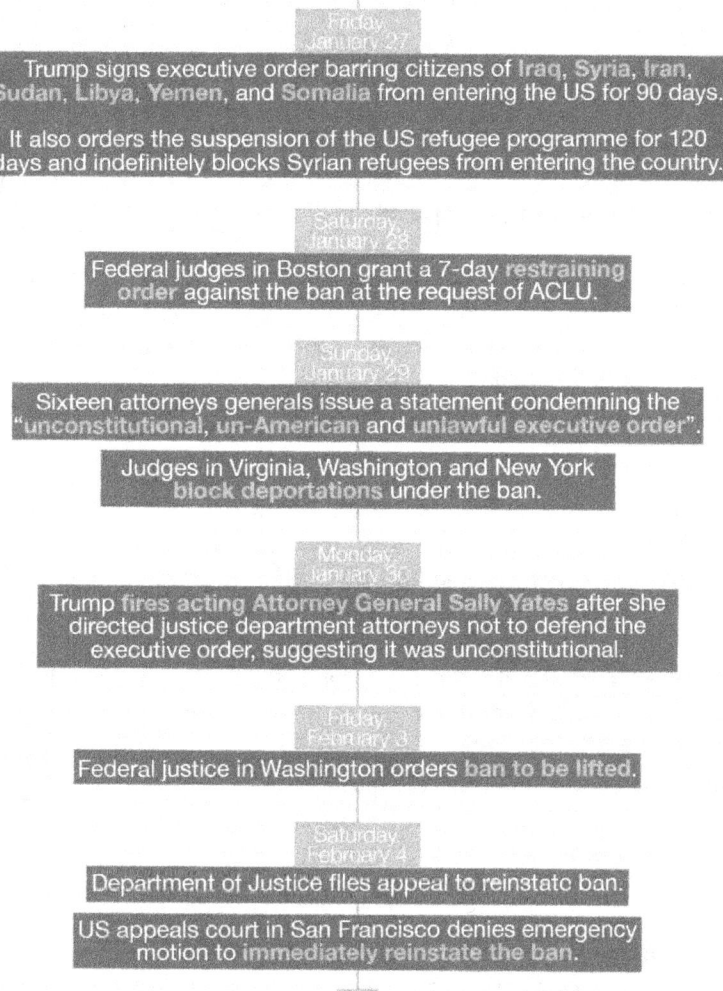

FEDERAL COURTS GIVE CONFLICTING DIRECTIONS ON TRAVEL BAN

Two different courts, on opposite coasts, ruled in opposite directions. A Boston federal court affirmed Trump's executive order as "bona fide"; a Seattle federal court enjoined it. Both spoke to requests for "nationally" effective rulings. Can federal courts give conflicting directions to government employees? Did HOMELAND predict this in their screenplays?

The Seattle decision overstepped the traditional boundaries of district court authority, especially when sister courts are ruling on the same issues. Both the Supreme Court and the Ninth Circuit warned against issuing a national order in just these kinds of cases.

Unlike state courts, federal courts enjoy the possibility of national reach in their decision. Due to the risk of conflicting decisions within the courts, venue-shopping by litigants (note how the ACLU, CAIR and the Attorney Generals aren't suing in any Trump states), and the interference with the executive branch of government in their daily duties, the Supreme Court established precedents — precedents being what constitutes "evidence" for lawyers about what the law says — to limit this problem from occurring.

First, the Supreme Court warned against issuing any relief not individually and specifically necessary to the plaintiffs before the court. Califano v. Yamasaki, 442 U.S. 682, 702 (1979). The Seattle judge's ruling goes way beyond that, trying to apply his order to people all around the world. It appears the Seattle judge thinks the people voted him President of the United States. Welcome to the ego of federal judges.

Second, the Supreme Court warned against issuing any such relief against the executive branch, especially in military, immigration, or foreign policy concerns, given how precarious such orders can threaten security, and interferes with day-to-day functions of the executive branch.

Noting that "neither declaratory nor injunctive relief can directly interfere with enforcement of contested statutes or ordinances except with respect to the particular federal plaintiffs," the Supreme Court warned against extending its reach beyond "the particular federal plaintiffs" in the case. Doran v. Salem Inn, Inc., 422 U.S. 922 (1975). The Seattle order tries to apply itself to millions of people around the globe. And folks think only brain surgeons look in the mirror and see God.

Third, as the Ninth Circuit, that governs the Seattle court, repeatedly ruled: a federal court should not issue rulings beyond its jurisdiction when other courts have also issued rulings on the matter. AMC Entm't 549 F.3d at 770. The "principles of comity" compel that a court should not grant national relief when doing so would "create tensions" with courts in other circuits and "would encourage forum shopping." The Ninth Circuit further reinforced that: "A federal court…may not attempt to determine the rights of parties not before the court". What kind of case was that the Ninth Circuit said not to extend your ruling beyond the plaintiffs in front of you? An immigration case. Zepeda v. INS, 753 F.2d 719, 727 (9th Cir. 1983); Nat'l Cir. for Immigration Rights v. INS, 743 F.2d 1365 (9th Cir. 1984).

The Supreme Court already reversed an order just like the Seattle order. In 1993, a few folks challenged the don't ask, don't tell restrictions on gays in the military. Shock, shock, they filed the suit on the west coast. Shock, shock, a liberal judge tried to convert it into a national injunction. Guess what happened? The Supreme Court reversed, issuing a stay of all parts of the injunction that "granted relied to persons other than the named plaintiff." Dep't of Defense v. Meinhold, 510 U.S. 939 (1993). Notably, that decision to stay the injunction was 9-to-0, unanimous. That is how obvious the precedents — the evidence of the law — is in this instance.

Just like every Senator looks in the mirror and sees a President, many federal judges look in the mirror and see a philosopher-king who the world should accept as a benevolent ruler. They aren't. His biggest name to fame has been controversial rulings and statements in the Amherst expulsion case and a black lives matter controversy. Judge Robart might make an interesting President. But America didn't elect him President. He's never been elected to anything. His judicial superiors are about to remind him of that.